Change Your Life In 5 Days

The Secret Formula to Live Your Dream Life

Prriya Kaur

This book in hindsight, reflects upon the journey of Ms. Prriya Kaur and the changes that have been brought by her in the lives of several individuals through her mentoring sessions and courses. To know more and redeem a course exclusively meant for the reader of this book, mail your purchase invoice to courses@prriya.com

CONTENTS

Acknowledgement

I would like to thank all of my colleagues, clients, and students who have contributed to this book.

It's all because of the strength that my family - my husband Sharminder Singh, my daughter Sharan Kaur, my son Harry Singh, my father Mukhtiar Singh, my mum Kulwinder Kaur, my mother-in-law Harjinder Kaur, my father-in-law Balveer Singh gave me, which enabled me to share up my thoughts, experience and knowledge in this book.

I would especially like to express my gratitude for my Mentor Mr. Jay, friends, Manjit Sahi, Sukhi Gill, Gitish Singla, Salma Ramzan, Dr. Toqeer Rasool, Sandeep Kaur, Nippy Singh, Zoe-May Ferries, Saeeda Khan, Palvinder Kaur, Gurjeet Kaur, John Paul Bryce and Chirag Jaitley.

"Although you have to travel the path of life on your own, the company of the right people make the journey worthwhile"

- Prriya Kaur

Preface

Starting things off…

Before proceeding ahead, take a moment to calm things around you by relaxing yourself and taking deep breaths for a few seconds. As you do just that, take a moment and ponder about what actually might have been in place that you came across this book. A book capable of altering your life for good and eventually setting you on your desired path of success.

Maybe it's a recommendation from an esteemed friend whom you look up to, maybe a trending thread or a post where the book is being praised. It can even be the title itself, with a peculiar meaning being conveyed to your brain and senses that instantly drowned you into a stream of questions.

Well, whatever the case might be, out of so many probable permutations and combinations that were happening behind the scenes (which we'll retrospect upon later in the chapters), you eventually got hold of this book. Just like so many individuals whom I've guided, mentored and counseled to bring about a change in their life, I believe that you also have the potential to achieve what you seek. And I am sure that you'd be amazed to see the outcome of adapting the methodologies and techniques which we'll be practicing throughout this book.

Would these five days be enough to bring about a change?

I often recall the moments where people came up to me and were initially skeptical about believing in a self-help system. They were astonished to see themselves at their desired spot. They even managed to overcome certain deep-rooted challenges which they thought they'd never be able to do away with.

As the saying goes, '*It all starts with a belief*'. So, I 'believe' that the aforementioned common question which pops up, should rather be '**Can** these five days or ways bring about a change?' Because right there and then you'd have thought to yourself, what I am about to put up and now you'll affirm to it that it actually doesn't matter if its five steps, five days, five weeks, or even years that are enough or possibly the go-to number that turn or shape your life the way you want it to be.

It all comes down to the question, do you have the will and determination to walk on that path of success? There have been instances where situations have flipped for good in a fraction of seconds. Obviously, there's a huge possibility of years of effort or smart work being there behind the scene and the result just came off. But ultimately, the penultimate stage before success has to be completed in order to build it up with character and stature.

Now coming back to the question '**Can** these five steps or ways bring about a change?' Well, if I've to simply put forth, '*you won't get to know unless and until you try*'. To avoid making it seem like mocking, I'd put forth certain points or facts that'll strengthen your thoughts on putting firm confidence in the phrase and eventually yourself.

I have worked with several new-age influencers, A-list celebrities, and various corporate honchos of top blue-chip companies and helped them to boost up their productivity, besides steering them to achieve their desired goals. I've compiled the entire knowledge and experience in this book, which are reflected in the paradigms spread throughout the chapters. What I'm today, is a result of incorporating certain techniques and I have to say that I've come a long way from being in a state of dilemma and lack of confidence to achieving what I once thought was out of my league. It may sound clichéd but *if I can do it, you can make it happen too!*

In fact, if we take a look at the life journeys of several accomplished individuals, in majority of the instances we'd find that they started from nothing and became self-made millionaires or billionaires. All they did was centered on having a belief in themselves or in what they were planning to do, and put all their time and energy in it, to make that happen or come true.

After thorough observations and analysis of these individuals, which I did through the interactions and sessions that I've had with them, I concluded notable common traits that they possess even if they are dealing in different walks of life. All this, in addition to what was mentioned previously, would be taken up by us every day for the next five days, implementing the handy approach of one step at a time.

'The moment you doubt whether you can fly, you cease forever to be able to do it'

- J.M Barrie

Over the course of time, you'll craft yourself in such a way that the strategies that we'll be going through would help you for a very long period of time, even if you stop using them. Just like when you learn to drive a car for the first time, it seems quite challenging but eventually when you're proficient at it, you can take it for a ride whenever or wherever you want.

For ages people thought that traveling through the air or flying overseas would be a distant dream. But in 1903, after years of trials, Wright Brothers gave us the first successful heavier-than-air powered aircraft. Although full-fledged commercial aviation and modern airplanes took a long while to come into the picture, that one instance was enough to shake the entire world and restore their faith in envisioning themselves to be taking a comfortable journey through the air.

The human mind has a tendency to generalize the experience or put everything in the same basket even if the situation or scenario was completely different and that too in a different time setting. This applies to good and bad ones, and usually in the cases of *'not so good ones'*. As we progress ahead, we'd shatter any futile pessimistic views that you have about the world and your surroundings and establish an optimistic perspective of looking at existing things and new interactions that you'd have.

The **potential** of the decade of '20s of 21st century

Every era or epoch has had its own set of challenges and opportunities. While some may argue that things are much tougher and degrading now due to the increase in competitiveness of modern society and negligence of values. The underlying fact is that, if one has the capability to utilize the resources at their disposal and make an influence through their work, this is the best time frame to be in. Undoubtedly on the face of it, we still have a long way to go when it comes to dwelling in a utopian setting. But at least to a great extent and in major parts of the world, we don't have to deal with the issues that threaten the fundamental meaning of existence that our previous generations possibly have faced.

With pivotal breakthroughs and improvements in technology, communication, transportation and plethora of such contemporary aspects like education, healthcare etc. the 21st century, especially the decade of 20s is going to cater to the league of opportunists who are ready to tap into benefits that their surroundings offer.

Thus, it becomes important to understand the mechanisms that are in place all around us, which are simultaneously shaping our lives and molding the way we perceive things in day-to-day affairs. This would enable us to resonate with other individuals and subsequently help in finding a niche for ourselves where we can excel and provide or produce something for which we can be rewarded. In this way we'd be doing what we like and also won't have to worry about our sustenance in the longer run.

Social Media is a great medium to do just that and has empowered many folks out there to showcase their talents, dexterity and products which ultimately promoted them to a great extent. But the catch or (the necessity just to say) here is that you'd have to be agile and just like every other triumph story, you'd also have to be consistent in building a brand for yourself or for your organization.

Therefore, it becomes equally crucial that you start right away as that would assure that your ingenuity does not get cluttered or overshadowed by the volume of ideas put forth by different individuals. Realize *'the power of doing it now'* and just jump right in.

"Success today requires the agility and drive to constantly rethink, reinvigorate, react, and reinvent."

– **Bill Gates**

About me and the foundation of P.S.A

"Find yourself, this is the beginning of all wisdom and happiness" - Prriya Kaur

I remember how fascinating the world of super accomplished people seemed to me at one point of time. Today it gives me immense pleasure to realize that now I'm in a position where I happen to interact with most of them quite frequently. It has been a long journey, and along with a blend of nostalgia, happiness and a whole lot of feelings that I experience when I recall each and every moment, a divine sense of faith in the approach towards life that I took, keeps rejuvenating me.

All the merry things and happenings that came across me over the course of the past few years, were indeed a result of a lot of efforts being put in by several related yet different domains pertaining to and surrounding my life. It wasn't always a smooth road at all though! Just like a lot of economically middle-class folks out there, my dreams were so big that it seemed they would always exceed my financial capabilities and I might not be able to achieve them throughout my life.

When I used to look at my cousins who were relatively well-off, I often asked myself what is that particular thing with them that they are so prosperous, so happy in their life whereas there's so much misery around me. I was in grade 8 when I came across a picture of the graduation ceremony of one of my cousins and it immediately popped up to me that one day I also want to study, pursue education and go to university like them. But the very next moment, the reality of my state of being at that time flashed in front of me. I started to ponder about all the expenses that would come in, the kind of education that I would require to enroll for further studies and many more such things that hindered my vision for the life of my dreams.

My grandmother used to say that whatever our condition is today, it's because of the things that we did in our previous life span, kind of like a result of our previous *'Karmas'* that we are facing presently. All these beliefs were so ingrained, that it seemed like maybe me and my family would have to go through the same melancholy for our entire life.

As time went by, I got married and became a mother as well. Although I was content to see myself in a new role where I was parenting my adorable children, I still felt a void deep down inside. And all this happened when I was quite young, the enormous number of responsibilities to look after a lot of things came onto relatively burgeoning shoulders!

I wanted to live my life to the fullest - drive nice cars, have an amazing place for dwelling, holiday internationally etc. But it felt as if everything came to a standstill and I would have to carry the pain of not fulfilling my aspirations with me forever. Eventually I found myself getting stuck and drawn into the ever-abominable loop of 'blame-game'. I started to hold my family, God and others responsible for all my distress. The environment around seemed to constantly mock me and eventually I began considering myself to be worthless.

As things started to become more and more monotonous, and I was desperately hoping for some magic, some opportunity to come my way, I got approached by a friend of mine all of a sudden. She suggested me to go for personal development sessions, where probably I can find a sense of relief and ease out the mental turmoil that I was going through. I had absolutely no clue what self-development was all about. But as I went through couple of resources, read a bunch of books, I started to get hold of the wonders that self-help and personal development can do in our lives. Something lit up in me, but unfortunately that fire extinguished to a great extent by a peculiar incident that happened after a while.

There was an opening for sanitization and cleanliness work in a nearby shop. I thought that I might be a good fit, since all this while, from the moment I got married and even at instances prior to that, I was really into homemaking. But to my surprise, they asked me about my educational background. I was like, what sort of qualification would it require to mop the floor or clean the store? Eventually, as I expected I wasn't selected for the job and it left an impact on me. I became upset and broken from inside and it all got added onto the pile of already sorrowful emotions.

Whatever the case might be, for some reason I started to hear a voice within me. And for the very first time, when I almost entered my thirties, I paid attention to what was being said by that voice. It echoed a deep-seated question and sought an answer for the same - *What do you actually want to seek in your life Prriya?* To which I replied, I want to study. I want to go to university and achieve the top rank over there. I want to have my own business. And most importantly I want to bring a change in the lives of people so that they don't have to go through the situations that I have been through.

With all my faith and determination, I asked my family and my parents if I could go and enroll myself in a university and pursue my studies from there. And to my amazement, they agreed! Perhaps my destiny was like - let's ease out something for her this time, because she has got a lot of challenges ahead anyways. And thus, my university journey started. But as always, and as I mentioned, there came a lot of obstacles ahead. This time it was again due to inadequacy of my education, that I had to grind really hard and it took quite a while for me to finally achieve what I always wanted to.

Another peculiar instance that I would like to share, panned out during the final days of university. I had to write down a citation as a submission for qualifying the end-semester exam of the university. I submitted the first draft to my tutor and his reply almost shattered me. He said that he hasn't come across such a pathetic work in the span of his 25-year teaching career. Interestingly the voice which I mentioned earlier, started to resonate again within me. It said, if you have come this far Prriya, you can go further as well. There's nothing that can stop you! Keep going ahead!

And guess what, I was heavily praised for the new citation that I wrote and curated and eventually received a medal for that as well. All the way through, I started to ask myself a few questions. One of them being, what actually made me accomplish something that I really wanted to have with me for so long? The answer I found out led me to recognize the notion and importance of having a strong, positive self-image, that also eventually shaped me into who I am today. The kind of identity that you have really makes a lot of difference, which we'll also be focusing upon later in the book.

Next, I discovered the power of the subconscious mind which gets unleashed when you start to love, believe, understand and hear yourself. This reminded me of the sayings of my grandmother who used to say that pray to God and he'll give you everything you wish to seek and take away your miseries. I realized over time that it is actually that divine element of thought, the voice that is present in everybody which can lead them onto the path of success. If you have the capability to dream, you also have the strength to make them come true. I've seen a lot of people who do not recognize the power within and go all their life cribbing about things not mending according to them. I pray that they awaken themselves and get to live a life that they have always wanted to.

Practicing meditation, checking your belief system, getting well-versed with your subconscious potential, hearing out your feelings, forming a confident and positive identity etc. are usually not taught in schools, colleges, universities and other conventional institutions. But it can all be learnt through books and various personal development resources. All the good qualities and the beautiful things which you tend to look for outside have their roots within you. So, if you want peace, prosperity, and wealth in your life, you must develop the habit of listening to yourself. The foundations of success would be laid from there and then only. Going all the way from being a semi-literate homemaker to an established entrepreneur, I reached a position where I achieved financial independence, became fully occupied and started remaining wonderfully joyous all the time. I understood that learning is an ongoing process, in fact even today I continue to learn every day from my surroundings and people around me.

With firm courage and determination, I overcame all my challenges and after completing my Master's in Business Administration (MBA, where I specialized in 'Leadership') from the world-famous *Edinburgh Napier University, Scotland*, I emerged as a successful Life and Business Coach, Entrepreneur and Counsellor.

From being in a state where I underestimated myself, to becoming confident of producing all the results that I wanted in life, I believe that you can also achieve the same or in fact greater levels of confidence and competence to create the results that you desire and deserve.

Helping people come out of their challenges has become my passion and I am truly happy pursuing it! Thus, I laid the foundation of *Prriya Success Academy* in Scotland, U.K, where there's a team of like-minded and passionate individuals who are determined to assist people in achieving big breakthroughs in their lives. Whether one's looking for some massive improvements in health, career, business, wealth, relationships, finances or personal life. The academy aims to guide individuals in moving closer to their dream life till they actually achieve it.

But since I really wanted to bring a change on a larger scale, I thought that I should put up all the knowledge and experience I gained through online courses and books. This would enable people not able to have a physical presence at P.S.A. get well versed with the ideologies and techniques. *'Change your life in five days'* is one such brainchild of just that, where together we'll embark upon a journey to lead you closer to your dreams and aspirations!

Here's my daily affirmation that I would like you to say to yourself before starting off each day –

I am born to succeed, the infinite power within me cannot fail. The divine law and order govern my life, divine peace fills my soul, and divine love saturates my mind.

Infinite intelligence guides me in all ways, God's riches flow to me freely. I am advancing, moving forward and growing mentally, spiritually, financially and in other ways.

I know the truth is sinking into my subconscious mind and will grow at its time, today is God's Day. I chose happiness, success, prosperity and peace of mind,

All I need is within me.

Gearing up for the change ahead

We're about to start our voyage for the next five days to reach the destination where you'll find a better version of yourself. Just as it is the case with any trip or journey, there are certain preparatory measures, here as well. We're going to brief ourselves up with a bunch of points as a prerequisite.

'Imagine for a moment that you were cherishing upon a dream, where you were in a position where you always wanted to be. You woke up the next day only to realize that what you felt is now actually your reality. What would it be like?'

As we came across the significance of doing things right at the moment. It's recommended that you visualize and think about it now. Ask yourself:

- How would you get to know that *'it'* finally happened?

- What would you see around you?

- What would your finances be like?

- What sort of leap would you have taken in your career?

- How does it feel to have finally made it?

- Who are going to be the people around you?

- Which part of the world or even space would you be at that point of time?

- How would you be adoring your relationships?

Proceeding step by step and implementing the routines in this book, you're going to vividly see these wonders happening in your day-to-day life.

Just pacify all the jarring thoughts and give a window to the positive vibes to settle within you through the practices and ideas in this book.

Though, the thing that you'd have to keep in mind is that patience is the key to success. As the famous saying goes, *'Rome wasn't built in a day'*, what you're thinking to ultimately achieve may come to you in a short span of time depending upon several factors. But you'd have to develop the trait of being patient at all times and you would've had to return to the book at instances during initial months. It's also said that success does not have a set recipe, just a bunch of ingredients are common. You'd have to understand that it's not a onetime spoon-fed meal, that after the consumption of which you'll become a champion of your race. Consistency and persistence are key elements which need to go hand in hand until they become a part you alter-ego.

Your future lies on what you do today. Every small action has a consequence, even if it's not noticeable to us but it gets registered as soon as it's done and the outcomes start to work behind the scenes. Evidently the results can be altered based on what you are putting in to shape them according to you, but then the efforts have to be in the right place and at the right time for real. And together we're going to figure out how to do just that…

We cannot choose our external circumstances, but we can always choose how to respond to them. – **Epictetus**

Taking the control of your Life

This must have happened to you many times previously that your decision was influenced by something or someone you considered significant initially, just to realize later that their presence was absolutely vague in the first place and it hampered your decision-making ability at that particular instance, where otherwise things could've been better if you went the other way.

First let's just recognize the fact that we all make mistakes at some point of time or the other and the most important thing to understand out of it is that it's necessary to learn from them and make changes accordingly. Otherwise, we'd be stuck in a constant loop and it'd be difficult to get out of it. Now coming back to what we were pondering upon, the straightaway conclusion that we can make out of there is that unless and until you take control of your life and stand by it, someone else would take charge of the driver's seat and would keep steering your life in the direction in which they feel like. You'd be swinging here and there only to realize that you need to siphon your life the way you want it to be.

The reason why I am putting this up is that most of the time people quit their development process half way through, thinking that it can't be done or it's too difficult for them to achieve. What they don't realize is that they might be just a step away from what they were expecting to accomplish, and in the longer run they might end up blaming different entities for not attaining it in the first place. This would only make things worse, and as it was mentioned earlier, it might throw one in the loop of dilemma and dwindle their self-esteem.

The way out is to get fully versed with one's senses and use their cognitive abilities whenever such a situation arrives. If you're the people's favorite choice of a listener i.e., someone who lends an open ear just to make them feel that their voice is being heard, then go by the philosophical phrase of *'listening to everyone's opinion, but following what your mind and intuition says'*.

Once you commit yourself to what you believe in, certainly after deliberate thinking, then you shouldn't back off.

Using this book to the fullest and to your advantage

As the title goes, we'd be taking a thorough look through the five steps, covering each one a day and figuring out the quintessential essence of a successful life that you envision, incorporating the associated values and traits simultaneously. Bit by bit, you'd be transforming into a better version of yourself and would also start feeling your perceptions and productivity change.

Although to extract the full potential that this book carries, it's recommended that you go through it when you're a bit relaxed and have comfortable space to practice certain mind programming techniques. Take your time, maintain a steady pace and feel free to turn back to the pages to refresh the contents in your mind. By the end of the next five days, you'll start to see the change in yourself, and you will be ready to tackle any situation that comes in your way. You'd also be on your way to join the ranks of the accomplished personalities, whom you've always looked up to and in no time would start to reflect a different aura in your surroundings.

Welcome aboard, let's kick start our journey with a very introspective approach that will be followed in the next chapter which paves your way towards being the person you always wanted to be…

A note from my daughter…

It's undoubtedly an extremely proud moment when you see your children flourish in life and attain a certain level of maturity that makes you wonder about the beauty of time. When they give you affection in terms of recognition and appreciation of your journey, it feels like you're on top of the world! I recently came across a note from my daughter, which she had penned down as one of her essays and it was lauded by her fellow mates and mentors at the high school which she used to go to. Without further delay, here's the exact note:

My Mom Is the Best

No little girl in Scotland or any other part of the world would be happy to see her hard-working mother distressed, confused and sad almost throughout the day. Well, as far back as I can remember, that is how I saw my so very affectionate mother on every day.

When I was around 7 years of age, I was always confused and wondering as to why my mother was suffering like that. It was not a pleasant sight at all. I was quite small at that time but was grown up enough to realize that this was not normal. I never found my friends' mothers so much stressed and sad.

Though it is over 10 years now, I still have distinct memories of my taking my mother's head in my hands and lovingly putting it in my lap, trying to console her while gently stroking her hair. At that age, it should have been the other way round. I should have been receiving those gentle strokes in my hair with my head in my dear mother's lap. But that was not to be so!

Fortunately for all of us, time runs so fast that our bad memories also become a thing of the past, sooner than later.

The picture mentioned above came crystal clear in my mind around 8 years later when I was proudly attending the Convocation function to award MBA Degrees to passing out students at the prestigious Edinburgh Napier University, Scotland, U.K. My mother looked stunning in the customary graduation gown and the cap, tassel and hood package. She couldn't hide her pride and joy, howsoever hard she tried. After all, her 'age-old' dream of wearing that square, mortarboard or Oxford cap had eventually come true.

Eight years had made a world of difference in the life of my mother. Her personality and outlook towards life had changed completely in this period. I distinctly remember that during those eight years, she was extremely busy all through the day. Her time-table for the day was always water tight but she efficiently handled her affairs. We never had any complaints against her as she was always there whenever her family needed her. And despite that, she had won prestigious medals at the University.

While I was watching my beautiful mother in awe during the above period, I was also building my own goals and aspirations to make my mother as proud of me as I was of her. I knew then and am aware now that it is not going to be an easy task. But after watching my mother's really tough journey during those years from close quarters, I feel confident that I shall, one day, make her proud of me!

I recall that in her times of distress, my mother did not have any opportunity to meet her parents. She could only talk to her mother occasionally. My maternal grandmother was a big moral support to my mother all through. She constantly counseled my mother to never give up; continue with her education, training and counseling and attend to her duties well at home. I now know how important it is for a woman to stay in touch with her mother, who would support the woman under all circumstances. I am determined to have a fantastic relationship with my mother all through my life. I know that she will always be there for me in my difficult and trying times.

My mother has treated me more as a friend in the last few years. She has been sharing the ups and downs in her life with me for quite some time now. She is keen to share her experiences as well with me, perhaps to teach me some important lessons in life. She also shares her critical learnings with me. I think it is all adding up to my balanced growth in life, even at this young age.

I have clear memories of the time my mother was denied even a low-paid job as she did not have the necessary qualifications. She felt badly hurt by this experience. But it did not deter her from taking some tough decisions in life. In fact, this incident made her a stronger woman. Soon she was able to acquire the requisite qualifications and that helped her join the renowned National Health Service (NHS). She worked for eight years in a well-known Scotland Hospital.

My mother was quick to pick up the basics of the mind science that she got to learn. She was a quick and willing learner. She also learnt the various techniques really fast and applied them on herself, to begin with. As she gained confidence, she benefitted more and more from her experiments with the mind techniques. Soon, she was using these techniques in her telephonic counseling sessions with her clients. Her confidence grew manifold when her clients too gained immensely and in quick time from the techniques taught and done by her with the clients. Her self-esteem also grew gradually. Our family life was also very pleasant and peaceful with all these changes.

My mum got her very own first car when she was just 33 years old. When I woke up to get ready for going to my school one day, I was startled to see an unknown car in our driveway. I ran down to find out more but was pleasantly surprised when I found my mum so very joyous right in the morning. With tears of joy in her eyes, she told me that she had bought that car with the money that she had earned for herself. Though it was not one of the best-known luxury cars, buying it with her own money made my mum so happy!

My mother soon joined a gym in the vicinity. She had her own personal trainer. She shared with me that this not only helped her improve her physical health but also built her mental health and overall well-being. It gave her more confidence and belief in her own self to achieve more in life by working hard. Today, she is mentally strong to overcome any challenges in terms of relationships, finance, wealth, self-esteem, confidence, business, health, career and anything else that you can think of. She is bubbling with joy and is ready to transform the lives of any number of people around the world by helping them on a one-to-one basis in coming out of their problems.

I am glad that my mum did not give up when she was in a really tough situation and instead chose to join the elite Edinburgh Napier University for doing her MBA with flying colors. If she had not made a wise choice at that time, I would have been deprived of a truly dynamic, robust and mentally strong role model for myself. She is simply amazing and I definitely look up to her and want to model her in my life.

Education and training have made my mother a wonderful trainer and a gentle human being who is true to her word. She is my role model forever. I cannot wait before I shout aloud and tell the world that My Mom Is the Best!

Sharan Kaur

Daughter (17 yrs.)

Day one/Step one

Finding the 'you' in yourself

Introspecting and discovering your true personality while unleashing the real version of yourself

'There was once a man who was known to be a champion at polo tournaments. The stature and the wealth that he had accumulated over the course of years was always looked up to by the people around him. But deep inside, he wasn't content. Always seeking for more, he wanted to make a mark in horse racing as well. Listening to the 'so presumed' wise advice from the stalwarts surrounding him, he even decided to change the horse that got him all the name and fame.

Months passed by, and he wasn't able to bag a single victory in the races nor was he able to fare well at the tournaments that he now occasionally played. Besides every materialistic possession that he had, everything started to fade away. Confused and tormented by what was happening, one day he suddenly stepped up on the saddle and without giving any thoughts or preparing for a journey, he simply rode away on his horse.

Days followed with no heads up whatsoever on the man. But interestingly one day a monk slowly walking along a road heard the sound of a galloping horse. He turned around to see the befuddled man riding a horse move towards his direction. When the man reached closer, the monk asked, "Where are you going?" To which the man replied, "I don't know, ask the horse" and with a pale look on his face he simply just rode away.'

Understanding the importance of influence

If we take a look at imperial legacy of the British empire, which at one point of time was subjected to a popular phrase, '*the empire where the Sun never sets*', we can study a lot of interesting facts and details about how the Englishmen started off as traders and eventually went on to rule major parts of the World.

The dominance over the Indian subcontinent was particularly talked about and often minute reflections of the sowed mentality amongst the region's inhabitants can be observed even today. Besides depicting their shrewdness, the tactics that they used to spread their reign demonstrated extensive brainwashing of the local, common men and women. This was a key element used in most of the countries. After manipulating many regional rulers and kings, and enforcing unfavorable policies upon them to annex their land, they targeted the rest of the dwellers from their grassroots.

Basically, the self-image of the masses was toyed around with. It was considered an elite thing to be and feel like British. The identity of the general residents was questioned and they were also compelled to go for goods that were brought up in the market by English traders. Interestingly most of the times, these goods had indigenous roots i.e., they were manufactured here and later were sold amongst the locals with the traders just merely acting as a middleman. The system of examination brought in the 19th century for getting the natives recruited for adding in service to the aid of British officers, was made to seem as if this was one of the prestigious and highly rewarding opportunities that can be sought after by them.

The reality was distant from what was being projected through. The ones who suffered realized it but couldn't help themselves in standing up against it. And those whose minds were still unaffected went on to be the rebels which heavily threatened the continuance of such immoral practices. The British administration was really shaken by the constant retaliation that was coming onto them in a very aggressive manner, which eventually after a chain of numerous events and several years turned out to be successful for millions of Indians.

But the unfolding of that event took quite a while, the reason being that British were really good at conniving and pitting the masses against each other.

Numerous attempts by the ones fighting hard for independence thus failed or had to be sacrificed in order to finally achieve that golden moment of freedom.

The main reason for taking a look back in time was not to refresh your history lessons. That would be a plus for sure though. But keeping quips aside, it was to retrospect and relate how impactful brainwashing or manipulating someone's self-image can be. We can observe a plethora of the effects of the activities of British at that point of time, as even today they are reflected in the personalities of the dwellers of the lands where they once had a presence. If we analyze extensively, it can be found that the seeds of imperialism that were once sown, still show their growth in the form of full-fledged trees of superiority amidst most of the habitants of those places. Their demeanor, the way of perceiving things is somewhere heavily influenced and was presumably passed down through the generations.

This leads us to talk about how to develop your Self-image and its importance in achieving your dreams.

Knowing your Self-Image

For most of us, self-image is like a reflection of ourselves in the mirror. But its literal meaning goes way beyond the observable reflection, to a bit abstract but impactful thought process. We have often come across instances where people who get overnight success or even the ones who seemingly are making a lot of money have to face a downfall associated with their eminence and prosperity. The reason is that they aren't able to cope with that sort of mentality which the 'successful' ones possess. Their self-image is crafted in such a way that they find it difficult to digest the fact about deserving that much money, fame or opulence.

The same can be seen in the cases of lottery where it's a common tendency that the winners quickly lose out on the amount won. This happens because they don't actually know what to do with or how to manage money in the first place, as they didn't imagine themselves to be in that position.

How you perceive yourself has a tremendous impact on you. You may think yourself to be tall, short, lean etc. depending upon your physical attributes and it's perfectly fine as long as you're content. Indeed, it's quite possible that you may want to look or feel a certain way, but it's important for you to realize that you are unique in different aspects. And in pursuit of how you want to portray yourself you shouldn't lose upon that unique trait, or feel sad about your current state of being.

Don't be influenced by what people around you say or make out your personality unless it's something that can actually make an improvement or would help you in the longer run. How to make out if something of such sort is worth it? Well, if you believe that by doing or implementing a particular set of actions that someone advises, you'd feel accomplished or a step closer to where you want to be, then go about it. Along with this there are many more factors to take into account like *'who that concerned individual is, or is it just a gossip that's being around you, with you in the picture'* etc.

But ultimately the key thing would be to not to do it, in case it makes you feel insecure. Because most of the time, people are just finding their insecurities within you and by what they say, your self-image gets manipulated.

Majority of what we put out during a conversation or discussion is based upon our subconscious mind. This determines our body language, tone and other characteristics. It's quite likely to be a possibility that, what we're saying and what we're projecting in terms of our physical presence at that moment, a completely different and confusing message is conveyed instead of what we intend to share.

So, it's important to have a strong sense of what your self-image is.

Only you know how to treat yourself better than anyone else. And by doing just that, you're sending out a message to others about how to treat yourself. So, the choice is all yours!

'A strong, positive self-image is the best possible preparation for success

– Joyce Brothers

The shrouded **Self-Image** and Sophisticated Success

Sometimes I tend to recount my experiences of dealing with renowned personalities. I found a stark difference between who they actually were and what they were trying to portray in front of the media and the public. I do this because whenever I have an interaction with any star or dignitary who's dealing with issues related to emotional imbalance, it helps me to figure out that deep seated issue which they have, which has led to that specific effect being dealt with on the surface. In majority of the cases the issue is a covered-up self-image, which as I mentioned, leads to a very contrasting persona of themselves.

It is quite obvious that no matter how many materialistic possessions like a luxury car, a mansion etc. one accumulates over a period of time, it won't be of any true purpose if there isn't any contentment inside. Yet it's intriguing to see so many people who are acquainted with this perceptible fact, still covering themselves in a glossy shell of showbiz where there's absolute hollowness inside. Adding to that, there are even more peculiar aspects to be considered, one of them being the fear of losing out on all this.

They are afraid that their so formed cover might blow up and their insecurities would be put out in front of the public, and thus most of the time they end up making a trial of fabricated ambience around themselves. As it is popularly called *'Fake it till you make it'*. It might work to an extent, but in the longer run it certainly has its consequences.

However, it is to be understood that, making a pretentious image or presence isn't only limited to the well-knowns or the wealthy. This also plagues the everyday workspaces, institutions where even for futile and small things, people tend to cover up to 'fit' or adjust themselves in the groups where the members are themselves in a void. Sometimes it can be the case and if it is, then it's best not to indulge in such a space. But in major occurrences, it is not a possible scenario even if it seems evident. Unfortunately, one tends to align their thoughts in such a manner that engulfs them in the barrage of questions related to their self-image. They thus end up faking it all, when it was not at all required in the first place.

It also gives me a bit of amusement when I look back upon my journey. How I started on a route to transform my professional and personal characteristics is something that drives me ahead in life and gives a sense of motivation when I need it the most. Coming from a very humble backdrop I felt extremely incompetent and dreaded about making it big in life. I realized that I had to channel my desire to be successful in order to get where I wanted to be. Eventually the pursuit yielded amazing results like a big house, all the luxuries that I wanted and most importantly, a beautiful relationship and a loving family.

Even though I achieved what I sought after to a great extent, deep within there was still a sense of incompleteness that made me wonder what exactly is it that would fulfill my purpose and make me happy? I realized that it was to bring a change in other's lives just like I brought in mine. To inculcate values and generate resources for the ones who need it most, so that they can excel in their fields. This became my mission and gave me an immense sense of happiness.

Although, I'm still not satisfied. I believe there is a lot to do in this regard, many more lives to be changed for good and I have this notion of excelling ahead in whichever domain I'm in – *'To be happy, but to never be satisfied'.* Because the moment you become satisfied, there's a huge tendency that you'll stop on your course. But it's equally important to be content and have joy flowing throughout your body, because ultimately that is what matters the most!

What leads to the **formation** of one's Self-Image?

As I mentioned earlier about the actions having a consequence, a similar approach can be drawn in the formation of your self-image. However, this time it'd be more about the actions of other people that have somehow shaped internal reflections of yourself, right from childhood. In an attempt to mold you into a better child or kid, besides encouraging you with constructive remarks on certain activities, it is quite likely that you were showered with discouraging or negative comments in the form of scolding. Although your parents, teachers might've said that "it is for the betterment of the kid, so that he learns quickly and gets prepared for the future", it is highly likely that this was to cover up for lashing out all their frustrations on you. Besides on the face of it, the reality might have been that they possibly would have treated you the way they would have been brought up all the way and thus the cycle had continued.

Even if for a second, we take those harsh words to be with a good intent, it has to be realized that children usually have a tendency to absorb whatever comes their way. And thus, it is highly likely that a negative self-image gets formed, full of low self-esteem and lack of confidence in doing certain things.

When one starts their schooling, things seem quite strange at first and it takes time to get used to the enforced methodologies. As the classroom sessions progress amidst the closed four-squared walls, the faculties at instances unknowingly criticize the students in a very unhealthy fashion, this leaves a profound impact on their overall development. Gradually puberty kicks in and there are a lot of changes physically and emotionally. Thinking about which in a bizarre way especially with a bunch of people going through similar commotions, makes everything seem like the worst place or state of mind to be in.

"Just as eating contrary to the inclination is injurious to health, so studying without desire spoils the memory, and it retains nothing that it takes in."

– Leonardo Da Vinci

It was tallied out in a research that by their mid-teens, majority of the school going students develop a negative self-image of themselves. And with time, if not looked into, it only gets worse.

As Noam Chomsky put up:

"The whole educational and professional training system is a very elaborate filter, which just weeds out people who are too independent, and who think for themselves, and who don't know how to be submissive, and so on – because they're dysfunctional to the institutions."

The common absence of curiosity and creativity in most of the individuals as they grow up, is a result of just that. When I started to draw a parallel comparison between Noam Chomsky's words and my life, I realized that there was this void that had to be filled. All my school life I was subjected to those boundaries which didn't let me explore beyond what was being taught with coercion. My interests weren't being talked about and that hindered my collective intellectual growth.

Ultimately after reaching that stage where I was ready to confront my negative self-image, I decided that it's time to make a few changes. I had already accomplished what I was seeking in the world outside my body, now I focused upon closing that small vicious gap that was making me feel empty. Once I took the leap, I started seeing changes in me, with the way I saw myself. That once 'semi-literate' version of mine, which was dismayed by how people treated me, started to alleviate and in due course of time, I got fully healed from within.

A really handy advice from the Stalwarts

A few years ago, entrepreneur Gary Vaynerchuk (*or Gary Vee as he's goes by*) while interacting with a diverse audience comprising of people from different walks of life, was asked, what is the most basic thing that one should have in order to get that uniqueness factor out through their presence?

He smiled and as always with his energetic aura coming straight onto them, he replied,

"Don't fool yourself in the belief of fake it until you make it"

The assemblage, majority of which were associated with entrepreneurship, got startled and intrigued at the same time. He elaborated it in a kind of similar fashion that was mentioned earlier,

"Literally if you want to let that uniqueness come out, then don't make or fake a different version of yourself or your brand. In the shorter run, it may work, but if you're on looking to see great results in the future, well they might just turn out too good to be true or in fact completely phoney"

Everyone nodded to what he said and he went on to cite the importance of genuineness in creating a strong identity for longer sustenance in a heavily competitive atmosphere.

Here's a key takeaway:

If you're putting in all your time and energy in hiding a negative image of yourself, it is quite likely to be a case that you're draining so many crucial aspects of your life which could've been channelized to lead you to your goals. You are possibly not living your dream life because of this and it's time to stop hiding your weaknesses. Rather it's important to work upon it and gradually that'll get you a step closer to your aspirations

As you go through the exercises in this lesson, you'll start to listen to your inner voice and perceive yourself in a completely different manner. You'll discover how to follow your instincts and with time you'll see massive changes coming your way.

The **different shades** of your Personality

Taking a look into our identity, at the core of our heart we'd find that we have certain attributes that make up a genuine version of ourselves – the original self.

But over the course of time with all 'yays and nays' about you being infused with your characteristics, a layer of negative self-image, the person whom you're petrified to let out publicly, gets formed.

So, to compensate for this, another layer is curated by us for being pretentious all the time. We 'presumably' try to gel-up with the people around us and cherish all that they can provide like love, materialistic things etc. This is the uppermost veneer that is donned by most of us in order to adorn ourselves. Rather what we're actually doing is to hide our negative self for the approval of others. And in this entire process we lose connection with the authentic version of ourselves.

Getting acquainted with your different selves

Let's dive into the pool of thoughts within you and have an insight on the peculiar traits of the three selves as they make an impact in your life. I will be putting up certain statements in the form of questions and you would be answering them being completely free minded and unbiased. This would help in lifting the cover of your pretending self, confronting your negative self-image (or feared self) by improving upon it and unleashing your real or original self. Just keep in mind that there are no 'best' answers - each question is plainly designed to raise your conscious acknowledgment of what is hindering you to be the authentic self:

'Thorough examination will do the healthy no harm, and it may bless the sick.'

- Charles H. Spurgeon

1. The imitated self: The person who you pretend to be

The image, through which you portray yourself as into the world is the imitated or pretend self. Often, this image is centered less on who you really are than covering how you think you are. Ask yourself the following questions:

• How do you like to be seen?

• Which feature of your personality would you like people to notice first?

• What is the most peculiar thing that everyone knows about you?

• If you're chasing after something and trying to prove it to the world, what would it be?

2. The Negative Self-image: The one whom you're afraid of

If someone mocks you with a name or phrase you don't associate yourself with, (for example, 'you skunk like creature!'), there is rarely any emotional impulse felt. But if something bothers and makes you sad, it's usually because in some way or the other you believe it might be legit.

Through the interactions that I have had in my sessions, I have found out that people often think in a manner where they totally deny that the negative traits they have, have got anything to do with them. When they ponder thoughtfully about it, they indeed come to realize that those traits were actually the ones they were truly afraid of.

One thing to consider that'll for sure help you in taking an honest overview of yourself:

Anything that you disapprove of in you or 'negative' traits are not exactly a part of you - they are associated with your negative self-image and were fed into you when you were a child. By discerning them wholeheartedly, you are about to let them go!

It can be difficult to confront and come face to face with our trepidations about ourselves - after all, it is quite likely you have tried to neglect them for a major part of your life. That's why, these questions are majorly going focus upon the things that reveal your negative self-image rather than your negative self-image itself:

- What are the traits that are contrary to existing ones present in you?
- Which clandestine information pertaining to you will only be found out after you die?
- Whom do you like the least as a person and what's the reason behind it?

(What we perceive is a projection of ourselves – what we most detest in others is what we don't like to reflect in our personality)

3. Your original self: A tryst with your authenticity

As you figure out the attributes or particular characteristics of your three selves, you are letting go and unleashing yourself to live a more beautiful life from the heart of who you really are – a life where you have full control of you and you harness the power of love.

Here are few points to know whether you are getting acquainted with the qualities of your authentic self or if you are stuck in the emptiness of your negative self-image:

- What are qualities that you possess at the moment?
- What would you do if there's nobody around you to bother?
- If it was all secure, what would you do differently?
- Who would you become, if you weren't afraid?

Reformulating your Self-image

Through the course of my life journey, I can recount many experiences where traditional methods or approaches to a positive thinking have not been very effective. Unless you're actually able to envision yourself getting better day by day, just seeing yourself in the mirror and doing positive affirmations for few moments won't be of much help.

To feel it vividly it, let's iterate it. If you were to stop all your activities for a moment and try hard to signal your heartbeat to speed up, it probably won't happen. But if you evocatively imagine yourself being on the stage in front of thousands of people, with the audience including some of the dignitaries whom you admire, it is likely going to be the case that your heartbeat increases.

These body triggers happen because:

The key aspects of how humans interact with their surroundings or react in a particular situation are based upon their habit and imagination, and they are far more dominant than logic and willpower at any given instance.

The truth is that your body is far more responsive to the vivid use of imagination than to a simple instruction to yourself. That's why how we perceive ourselves in our thoughts is really crucial and related to how we are living our lives in reality.

This instance as a matter of fact is quite well know - In the early 1970s Maxwell Maltz, a plastic surgeon, noticed that changing the physical appearance of his patients often made a dramatic increase in confidence and sometimes even a holistic change in personality.

However, it made no psychological alteration whatsoever in the personality of some of his patients, even though the physical changes were quite commendable.

He reached to a conclusion no matter how much cosmetic correction is made in the external appearance of a patient, it is of no use if their internal self-image is weak, or, as he mentioned, when they were 'scarred on the inside'.

Thus, to bring about a change in their lives as well, he advised those clients to follow a simple visualization technique that resulted in a magnificent change in their self-image.

To his amazement, it yielded equivalent or sometimes even more beneficial results than actual surgery. By suggesting his patients who had developed a negative self-image over the course of time, to continuously imagine themselves as ideally as they wanted to be, he noticed that they became more content and were in a state of peace within due course of time.

A **smart mind** to influence self-images

A really amusing yet quite plausible incident strikes me when I talk about how a small initiative can make big changes or rather can influence many minds by making them introspect their self-image.

I was once having a word with my friend, and suddenly her son walks in with a form that was supposed to be used for an activity assigned by his institute to gather collections for old age homes. Although her son was really enthusiastic and full of confidence when it came to interacting with people or addressing mass gatherings, he was a bit anxious this time as he had never done anything like this before. He was bothered about what is going to be the response from his neighbors and others when he asks for donations, door to door. My friend immediately came up with an idea and she wrote her monetary contribution along with her sign. Obviously she gave the amount she mentioned in the list on the page, and told me to do the same. Then she got hold of a few of her colleagues who also did the same thing. By doing so, almost 10 sections out of 40 on the list got filled and that too with decent individual contributions that were written as well.

She told me later that the very next day her son went out to get donations from the neighbors in the vicinity and the boy ended up getting the entire list filled with a decent amount being contributed by each household or local store that he went to. We both laughed and appreciated the methodology used which touched the self-image of the remaining 30 individuals who didn't feel like projecting themselves as less charitable than the existing 10 contributors.

This was indeed a really useful and clever way of directly reaching out to the self-image of numerous persons!

There is a famous incident related to Picasso when he was asked how some of his creations were purely based on sand-art. He replied, he visualizes and sees his subject in the frame full of sand and while he's making his art, he removes every particle off from what is supposed to be the center of attraction.

Reformulating your self-image is very similar to trying less to be the version you think you could've been and directing your thoughts more to realize the virtues of the person you really are.

You must go through this simple exercise at least once every day for a week and you will allow your self-image to easily infuse with your authentic self...

REFORMULATING YOUR SELF-IMAGE FOR SUCCESS

1. Sit in a comfortable place and take a while to relax and breathe deeply. As your body de-stresses and settles in the ambience, you'll find it easy to streamline your thoughts.

2. Now, visualize another version of yourself standing in front of you. This is the most genuine 'you', the alpha version i.e. the authentic self.

3. Take some time to cherish the moment with your authentic self. Carefully observe the way the 'authentic you' walks, talks, smiles, senses things around him and breathes. Imagine how he would interact with others, how he tackles problems, and goes for resolutions besides focusing on your ambitions.

4. Now, step in and synergize with your authentic self. See through the eyes of your alpha version, hear through its ears, and experience how enchanting it feels to live life as your authentic self!

5. At last, conclude your reformulation session by taking a minute to fantasize about how productive your life will be as you live more and more as your authentic self. You can imagine yourself being present with an original you in any situation from your past, present and future. (Do this for the next five days)

Closing our day and climbing up the ladder with our first step

When you'll start to live like your authentic self, it will become much easier to act consistently with that version of yours.

As soon as you commit yourself to something, the rest of you will align with it. Instead of affixing yet another image or limited personality onto your definition of 'self', the activities you have done today, will open up a window for greater possibilities and increase your potential.

It is a commonly observed fact that the ones who are truly successful, are the ones who've reckoned their flair - they don't feel awkward when they think about their uniqueness. Although aligning your self-image with your authentic self may not be the solution to every problem of life, it will enable you to go about your life more enthusiastically. As the *'perceived you'* and who you really are resonate more with each other, even before you see any changes in the outer world coming your way, you'll tend to be truly proud about yourself.

And as I've figured out for myself, the more you are content from inside, the better your life will become on the surface.

When I have fears that I may cease to be

Before my pen has gleaned my teeming brain,

Before high-piled books, in charactery,

Hold like rich garners the full ripened grain;

When I behold, upon the night's starred face,

Huge cloudy symbols of a high romance,

And think that I may never live to trace

Their shadows with the magic hand of chance;

And when I feel, fair creature of an hour,

That I shall never look upon thee more,

Never have relish in the faery power

Of unreflecting love—then on the shore

Of the wide world I stand alone, and think

Till love and fame to nothingness do sink.

- John Keats

I want you to congratulate yourself for taking and coming one step closer to your dream! Just know you are unique - there is no one who has ever walked the face of this planet who can do things exactly the way you do. You're unique in your own ways and over the next five days, we'll identify those unique traits and find out ways in which you can benefit from them by sharing your qualities with the world.

Looking forward to taking you a step further tomorrow!

Prriya Kaur

"It's not what you say out of your mouth that determines your life, it's what you whisper to yourself that has the most power!" — **Robert T. Kiyosaki**

Some heads up for the next day*: How would you like it if you can step into any state of mind you want to be in at any given instance? We're going to discuss the tips that'll help you take control of your emotions and command your brain, thereby making you the master of your emotions, mind and body that in turn would affect everything in your life...*

Day two/Step two

A tête-à-tête (conversation) with your brain

Getting fully acquainted with your thoughts and channelizing them to get best results

BEFORE STARTING OFF WITH TODAY

● **Take a while to go through the Self-image Reformulation exercise from day one**

● **Go through this daily affirmation:**

I am born to succeed, the infinite within me cannot fail. The divine law and order govern my life, divine peace fills my soul, and divine love saturates my mind.

Infinite intelligence guides me in all ways, God's riches flow to me freely. I am advancing, moving forward and growing mentally, spiritually, financially and in other ways.

I know these truths are sinking into my subconscious mind and will grow after their kind, today is God's Day. I chose happiness, success, prosperity and peace of mind,

All I need is within me.

1. Sit in a comfortable place and take a while to relax and breathe deeply. As your body de-stresses and settles in the ambience, you'll find it easy to streamline your thoughts.

2. Now, visualize another version of yourself standing in front of you. This is the most genuine 'you', the alpha version i.e., the authentic self.

3. Take some time to cherish the moment with your authentic self. Carefully observe the way that the 'authentic you' walks, talks, smiles, senses things around him and breathes. Imagine how he would interact with others, how he tackles problems and goes for its resolutions besides focusing on your ambitions.

4. Now, step in and synergize with your authentic self. See through the eyes of your alpha version, hear through its ears, and experience how enchanting it feels to live life as your authentic self!

5. At last, conclude your reformulation session by taking a minute to fantasize about how productive your life will be as you live more from your authentic self. You can imagine yourself being present with an original you in any situation from your past, present and future.

Once there was a free bird. She floated in the sky, catching midges for lunch, swam in the summer rain trickles, and was full of joy like many other birds. It all felt like a blessing and she totally enjoyed the company of other fellow creatures.

But she had a habit: every time some event occurred in her life, whether good or bad, the bird picked up a stone from the ground. Every day she sorted her stones, laughed remembering joyful events, and cried remembering the sad ones.

The bird always took the stones with her, whether she was flying in the sky or walking on the earth, she never forgot them. Years passed, and the free bird got a lot of stones, but she still kept on sorting them, remembering the past. Over the course of time, it was becoming more and more difficult to fly, and one day she was unable to carry the burden of the stones.

The freedom that existed some time ago, started to fade away and she could not walk on the earth besides being unable to make a move on her own. She could not catch midges anymore; only rare rain gave her the necessary moisture. But for some reason, she bravely endured all the hardships, guarding her precious memories. Other creatures and birds around her were baffled by her strange demeanor, as they were flourishing in nature, while she was going through tremendous difficulties, which were a result of her own deeds.

After some time, she died of starvation and thirst. Only a pitiful bunch of worthless stones were left behind, which reminded other birds of her for a long time.

A HOT CUP OF TEA

You must have noticed that it's usually a thing with celebrities, musicians, athletes etc. that they simply transition themselves into their charming and energetic persona, regardless of whatever state of mind they were in prior to their show or performance. Have you ever wondered how they bring about this immediate transformation?

This also used to be the case with the members of the popular band of the 70s, Led Zeppelin. Although they were known for being at the center of many outrageous tour shenanigans during the 1970s, including trashing hotel rooms and throwing TV sets out of windows, things mellowed out altogether over the decades. When asked from the front man, Robert Plant, about how they change their state of mind or if there's any pre-show ritual that they do in order to make that transition happen, he simply replied that he prefers to get ready for the performance with a cup of hot tea and freshly-pressed shirts and slacks that he ironed himself. He believes that this helps him get "in the mood", kind of like a 'switch' or a 'button' to get him into the desired frame of mind.

Today we're going to take a look at how you can master your emotions and channelize your thoughts to transition yourself into whatever state you want to be in a given situation. Be it reflecting confidence or radiating charisma wherever you go, you'll learn some really handy techniques, which to your amazement, would be really simple to practice yet the results that they'll yield would be able to back you up in any complex scenario and would stay pertinent for a long time to come.

Understanding temperamental states

You quite likely have come across an incident which was also spectated by someone else, and later you discovered that their take on it or experience of it was completely varying from yours. What could've been in function behind the scenes that you both felt things so differently, despite being at the same place and at the same time?

Let's take a case where people respond differently to depths of water bodies-some people won't even take a dip in the pool or swim in it, while some go for tremendous depths like deep sea or scuba divers even at instances beyond their physical capabilities. The difference in both the cases is because of the temperamental or emotional states you are in at the time. Love, anger, confidence, fear, apathy and curiosity are all emotional states.

Throughout any day, we're constantly swaying across different states of mind and each of them is just as unique as our fingerprints. The technical definition of emotional state is usually put up as 'the sum total of all the neurological processes occurring within one's body at any given point of time'. To put it simply, an emotional state is equivalent to the mood one has in response to a particular situation or in general at any instance.

We've all been through various kinds of emotional states. Sometimes we've felt depressed, angry or anxious. The other times we have rejoiced being in productive states, full of confidence, optimism and astuteness.

It thus becomes crucial to know about temperamental or emotional states because:

All human behavior is the result of state.

The best result of anything that we do or someone else does, only comes when there's a presence of an excellent emotional state when that activity is being carried out.

Today, you'll learn how to strategize your mind to get into any state you want in any situation where you'll need it the most.

What causes feelings to emerge?

Initially it seems that how we feel at any given moment, is directly related to the events happening around us. Something happens in the surroundings and our reaction to it depends upon the change in our emotional state. If we take an example, let's think for a second about someone or something you are extremely attracted to or attached with. Now imagine that thing or person just comes in front of you. In most of the cases we'd find out that our state of mind gets altered! As a matter of fact, a lot of us are completely oblivious of how our feelings generate and reorient from moment to moment. This happens because of an internal process that comes into function in the space between occurrence of an event and our response to it.

The mechanisms of our body

Some of the ways in which we're frequently influencing our state, correspond to the manner in which we take the charge of our body. Transformations in our stance, way of talking, breathing and facial expression, all work upon our feelings and behavior. It all depends on how we put our body in the systems around us. If we condition it to respond in an unconventional manner, it will be a completely different experience altogether of existing in those systems.

Relating it with an example, I would like you to recount an experience of yours when you became really nervous – presumably before delivering a speech in front of a large audience, giving a presentation at work, or before asking a question which you think would have made you look weird amongst the other folks present around you.

TAKE A PAUSE

And go through this small exercise - place your feet firmly on the floor, wherever you are and move your shoulders a bit back. Smirk for a while and take a deep breath. Now try to imagine that uncomfortable situation without changing your posture. Keep your shoulders relaxed, your feet fixed on the ground and your teeth shining!

If you followed through what was just mentioned, you would have noticed that either your feelings about the situation changed or you're no longer able to think about it in the same way.

The stress that builds up in our muscles, feeling of nervousness or its contraries i.e., relaxation, sturdy body posture, etc., all have an impact on our states. At times when you are tense, your body releases certain chemicals which are totally different from the ones which get produced when it's relaxed. That's if you perceive things differently in a better fashion internally, your overall external personality radiates a positive and strong message.

The reflections happening within

Now some of the determining factors which shape our thoughts from moment to moment, are in turn based upon the images we make in our minds and the way a conversation pans out with ourselves in our head. We address these pictures and sounds as internal portrayals, and they are just that - reflections of reality, not the reality itself.

Your internal renditions of actuality are peculiar to you – the way you comprehend the world around you. They are just like a globe. But as is the case with any other model of the world, they are not accurate and packed with presumptions, modifications and deformations. That's why two people going through similar scenarios, may put their experiences in a completely different fashion. As Descartes, the father of modern philosophy, put it - "Different eyes see the same thing different. This is what is called an opinion"

'Miracles happen every day, change your perception of what a miracle is and you'll see them all around you.'

- Jon Bon Jovi

Your mind as a movie theatre

The way I look at it, everyone has got the ability to visualize. To demonstrate it right away, give your take on these questions:

1. How does your smartphone look? What is its color? Does it have a headphone jack?

2. When was the first time you sat in an airplane? What was the destination of the journey? How cool was the overall ambience?

While answering these questions, it is quite likely that you imagined that particular moment or object and a bunch of images flashed right in front of you. Now, for the majority, these pictures will not be in 'high definition' and that's a perfectly normal thing. If those internal images were like a carbon copy of what we see in the real world, you wouldn't be able to differentiate between them.

In a similar way, we all possess the quality of talking to ourselves and creating sounds in our mind and sometimes, we can use it to our advantage. To feel it out, think of a song which you enjoy listening to or any form of music that makes you groove. Recall the sounds that you heard on a beautiful morning you woke up to, the birds chirping or remember the voice of someone you adore especially when they were complimenting you.

On the contrary, there might have been instances where you had a tiff with someone and even after a long while you were feeling really uneasy because you kept pondering about the inconsiderate things which they said to you.

Let's try something to understand our emotions better...

Imagine you're going to a club for the very first time. Visualize yourself standing awkwardly in one corner of the club because you haven't been to any before. You do have a bunch of friends, who are frequent visitors, and they asked you a few times as well to join the fun with them, but now they are so engrossed in their thing that they almost forgot about you. The music in the club is too loud and possibly the one which you don't often listen to. If you were to go to that club again… How likely is it going to be and with the same company of friends?

Now, imagine that even if you're going for the first time, you're confident and carry a charm with you that keeps on drawing the people towards you. You enter the club and eventually find yourself to be the center of attention of the entire gentry present inside. The DJ starts playing your favorite tunes and you simply light up the dance floor.

How cool does it seem to be now, and would you be hanging out in the same club more often?

If you felt any variation at all between those two situations, you'll be able to relate how the nature of your internal reflections shape the quality of your life. In spite of this, most of the time, people become so keen to surround themselves with movies or web series they'd like to watch instead of the cluster of images they play in their mind. That clearly demonstrates that in such cases, their brain takes the charge of their life instead of them firmly grasping it and building their thoughts accordingly.

A while ago I had an interaction with a movie star who was afraid about missing out on things happening around her or as it's popularly called these days 'Fear of Missing Out or FOMO'. After having a brief conversation, a few sessions were scheduled where I counselled her and after practicing out certain mind conditioning exercises, she was eventually able to overcome all her anxieties. What we did was all about analyzing and understanding the formation of images and related sounds that she made in her mind, and it was quite evident how she could generate profuse feelings surrounding her fear in just a matter of seconds.

Whenever she came across any post of her friends over the social media, where they were enjoying lavishly or possibly getting themselves a new car, a house etc. she started to think she is not being involved in such occasions, and even though she had almost every luxury one can think of, she was afraid that people won't be pleased with her because she doesn't own that particular version of that thing and many more such futile materialistic possessions around her.

She said to herself a string of things like, "Look at them, they have got the latest model of this car and I don't have it". After thinking for a while, she again whispered, "I'm not going to get work in the industry anymore, because I don't hang out with these guys that often" and "My husband is not going to appreciate me because I don't have that figure anymore as this young actress."

The reality was that she was one of the most reputed and successful actresses in Hollywood with a very caring husband, who was rather worried about his wife not coming to peace with her mind. It is understood that the exuberant world of movies and all the related starry stuff is quite competitive and it is a likely scenario that one might actually get swayed by all the flashy aspects of things. However, there are numerous examples of celebs as well like Keanu Reeves, who have to a great extent, distanced themselves from all the buzz, and have instead focused upon entirely their work, besides being fully down to earth all the time.

It was about time that she overcame this. I told her to first be at ease with herself and then vividly ponder upon these thoughts – *'the beautiful life she has had up until now'*, *'the loving family and fan base that she has'*, *'the accomplishments that she has had up until now'*, *'the supportive friends that she likes to hang around with in the personal and professional sphere'*. Then I asked her to actually visualize all this, when she feels even a tinge of anxiety.

After a period of time, not only she finally conquered her fear, but also started to appreciate and feel good about herself and the achievements that her friends were bagging.

And guess what happened. She actually ended up increasing her net worth by a significant margin the very same year and signed up for a big project that went on to winning several awards.

The crux of all this is:

You can get the pivotal control of your life, as you develop the ability to take charge of the way you perceive abstract thoughts in the form of images and sounds.

Let's try one more fun activity. Recall about someone who is extremely irritating or someone who constantly keeps pestering whenever you come across them – imagine their face in front of you. Now as you've come face to face with their image in your thoughts, ask yourself:

- Is the image bouncing back and forth or is it still?
- Are you making it in front of you, at the back of your head or towards your sides?
- Is there a particular setting of that image? Like what's the backdrop etc.?
- What about the colors? Does it have any Instagram filter on?
- What is the size of the image? Is it small or huge?

Now let's toy around with the image or reflection you've formed in your mind, of that person. Make the following adjustments or modifications and pay attention to what happens:

TWEAKING THE IMAGES IN YOUR MIND

1. Remove any filters that you've put over the image and make all the colors vanish away to make it seem like an old black-and-white photograph.

2. Decrease its size until it becomes extremely small.

3. Stop the motion of the image frame in case it's moving so that it becomes stationary.

4. Move the picture quite far away so that it's exactly in front of you.

5. Make the nose of the person like Donald Duck's and give its characteristics like big eyes, a blue cap etc.

6. Hear their voice in your head. Then change the texture of the sound coming your way to that of Darth Vader's, quite deep and intense. Now again alter the pitch so that it seems like Donald Duck is talking literally.

As you change your internal reflections, you tend to reformulate the way you feel or perceive things. How do you now go about the interaction between you and that person in a new way? What do you think about the new terms that can possibly develop between you both? It's quite likely to be the case that now you don't feel frustrated when you think about them. The next time when this person meets you, the way you both would think about each other would be very different. It also means that the way you would communicate with each other would mold the fundamentals of your relationship for good.

The concept that we're talking about here is:

The pictures that are large, glowing and striking generate greater emotional intensity than those that are dry, pale and placed far away.

Moving ahead, let's discover how we can manipulate our memory to our advantage by going through another technique, called *'detachment'*:

1. Remember any unpleasant experience of yours.

2. As you think about it, what sort of images wander across your mind? Imagine stepping out of yourself so that you can see those images clearly.

48

Draw yourself off from that image and visualize yourself moving slowly away from it as you think. By doing so, you reduce the intensity of the emotions that the image was triggering. Basically, you detached yourself completely from it in your mind.

Now taking things on a positive note, let's flip the process by the practicing the technique of 'attachment':

1. Remember any moment where you felt extremely happy and imagine what was it like. Let the images form vividly in your mind.

2. After the images start to take a proper shape, get engrossed into them so that you start to feel that moment through your body as if you're existing in the exact same place and at the exact same time.

3. Increase the size of the image, amplify the sounds and increase the feelings of ardor. Ultimately, you'll find out that you can maneuver your feelings about memories - to reduce the intensity, step out and move back; to increase the intensity, step in and make it bigger.

Not long ago, I was a guest panelist at one of the conventions where a topic about the importance of finance management in contemporary lives came up. One gentleman put up a question with me where he wanted to know how he can overcome the dread of a financial loss in his business that he suffered recently and eliminate all the commotion that's preventing him from making any more investments to grow his operations.

I immediately replied with a question and asked him to describe what sort of images form in his mind when he recalls that moment. He said that he sees the market charts going down, he visualizes himself getting anxious about his investors etc. I was easily able to make out that he was attaching or associating himself with the pictures that he created in his mind.

I told him to pull himself back from the illustrations that he formed (detach) until he felt that he had moved himself completely out of the equation by diminishing the size of images and fading the colors away. There was an immediate sigh of relief. I also advised him that in case such thoughts ever come back, it'd be best to simply detach or dissociate himself from them. A few weeks later, I got an email from him citing that he had expanded his business activities and as a result made commendable profits in that financial quarter!

You can use this following summed up table to your advantage

Reducing and getting over distressful memories:	Augmenting encouraging and positive memories:
* Move away or pull yourself out of the pictures (detach)	* Immerse yourself completely in the pool of images (attach)
* Remove all the motion from it and fix its position	* Make a sequence of these pictures like a film
* Diminish it and put it far away	* Increase the size of images and bring them closer
* Fade off all colors from it and reduce its photo quality	* Fully enrich them with colors and make them vibrant
* Lower the volume of sounds and make them inaudible	* Increase the volume and amplify the ambient sounds *(unless it's a serene memory)*

Our internal reflections have got a lot of potential and can even flip the entire situation by turning an underdog into a champion. A couple of years ago an 'E-sports athlete' came up to me and mentioned that he slowly started to believe in a conviction that almost all the top-tiered competitive gamers are using hacks and unfair means to maintain their position in certain leagues and tournaments. Although he was instructed by the counsellors of the organization that he played for, to imagine himself clutching (or winning) difficult in-game situations, he wasn't able to convince himself that he can actually beat the top leaderboard guys by fair means.

Rather, he now became anxious about maintaining his position in the tournament. Upon hearing from him how he visualized the situation, I figured out that he wasn't truly experiencing the moment as he detached himself from the image, standing outside of it all the time. Basically, the message that he sent to his subconscious mind indicated that he was winning the tournament through someone else's eyes.

As we discussed further, I got to know that he was making enlarged and vivid images of his competitors. I simply advised him to get fully engrossed (attached) in the picture of winning and reduce the size and shape of the one he formed when he thought about his competitors.

In a matter of days, he was manifesting tremendous confidence and eventually went on to clinch one of the top spots on the tournament's leaderboard.

To put it concisely:

How you feel from time to time or in a given situation depends upon the manner you use your physical senses and the relevant illustrations or images along with sounds that you make mentally within.

As you're aware now, how to influence your state, you don't have to worry about others or various sorts of things to make you perceive things in a particular fashion. By taking the full authority of the visuals in your mind, the opinions that you form about yourself (and how you form them), and the way you respond to your body, you can now select the feelings that you want to experience in any scenario.

Interpretations of your own voice

Sometimes a few nitpicking remarks made by the wrong person at the wrong time can pour cold water on your entire enthusiasm and plans that you have in your mind. The best example straightaway points to the commentator inside you, the one who dwells in and reaches out every single part of your consciousness. How you communicate with yourself has an intense influence on your state of mind.

Think about a time when you made a small blunder. Carefully examine the way you spoke to yourself at the point of time. Did you say, 'Ah it's alright, next time I'm going to be careful!', or was it on the completely opposite side of the spectrum - ' How can you be so absent-minded? You better know what consequences are coming your way!' or 'When would you stop making the same mistake again and again?'

Keeping everything aside, what was the tone of your voice? Did you go too harsh on yourself and it sounded like the end of the world? Or was it gentler and saintlier?

Successful entrepreneurs find the balance between listening to their inner voice and staying persistent in driving for success – because sometimes success is waiting right across from the transitional bump that's disguised as failure.

– Naveen Jain

A lot of individuals think that just because they are hearing something inside their head, they have to pay extensive attention to it. What I rather believe, is that the feedback that you receive from within has to be benefiting and supporting. However, if the criticism coming from your inner voice is not constructive, then you must consider going through this exercise.

THE CONSTRUCTIVE CRITICISM

1. Take a pause for a while and have a conversation with yourself in that cynical voice, pointing every flaw out and with an irksome intonation.

2. After that, observe where that voice comes from. Is it inside your head or anywhere else in your upper body? Is it echoing or is it just a plain one?

3. Now stretch your hands and focus on your index finger

4. Wherever that voice was coming from, make it go all the way through your arm to the tip of your index finger, so that now it blabbers to you from there.

5. Finally, change its pace and texture. Make it sound funny, or play around with its tone so that it seems like any favorite cartoon character of yours is talking with you.

You would feel for yourself that the conversation with your inner voice would seem soothing!

It is to be kept in mind though that even if you've learnt to alter the characteristics of the voice in your head, you have to realize that the intention of that inner critic would always be for your good - to prevent you from going the wrong way and help you get back on track. However, it is equally true that for any sort of criticism, it has to be constructive to be of any good.

Think about a time when you were a kid and were made to learn new things. If you were continually being yelled at every time you made a mistake, chances are that you would've had a hard time learning all things being taught to you and possibly you'd have drained all your confidence. Instead, if you were encouraged and explained things properly without any anxiety or emotions about your future attached to you, chances are that you wouldn't have to read this book in the first place!

Anyways, keeping all the puns aside, let's do one more exercise:

1. Recall a moment when you did something wrong or off and you heavily scrutinized yourself. Review exactly what went through your head in the form of those voices.

2. Now think, how can you convert the message so that it sounds encouraging?

3. Re-live that particular moment and instead of what you said to yourself at that time, constructively analyze and give feedback to yourself this time.

From now on, carefully observe how you talk to yourself. Modify the tone of the voice, change the words and try to develop a sense of 'learning and improving' through what you say to yourself.

Visit PSA's social media handles and inbox us with this book's purchase invoice. You'll be given complimentary access to a course valued at 99 Pounds

The essence of all of it is:

Your choice of words defines you. Choose them correctly and you'll be the best person one has ever come across, especially for yourself!

Manipulating your feelings whenever you want to

We think that it would be best to control our state of mind and change it whenever we feel like. Indeed, it's necessary to have a grip on your states, but instead of altering them by yourself, it's rather more beneficial to maintain consistency with them, so that they get modified automatically whenever it's most needed.

Notable and serial entrepreneurs follow routines and do certain mind exercises every day, not to run their ventures on a daily basis. They do it so that they can impulsively transition into their alpha states whenever they need it the most, for example during pitch decks, investor meets, financial losses etc.

In order to provide you with an experience of conditioning your mind and body for achieving more, we'll take a look at two easy to practice techniques that'll pump up your assertiveness in any instance. If you feel like it, you can revisit these and switch to the feeling you want to experience.

As you get used to these exercises, you'll see that you will inculcate changes at a pace that you're comfortable with, which will ultimately make you more confident.

It doesn't matter if you get that boost instantly or gradually as you practice. What matters is that you'll master yet another technique to your advantage!

Let's start off. Go through each step, one by one and as you become familiar with it, get ready to rock and roll!

BOOSTING YOUR CONFIDENCE IN A JIFFY

1. Taking support of your backbone, place your head high and sit in a comfortable and relaxed position, loosening your shoulders. Think of a bright and shiny thread running all the way up through your back and neck connecting you straight to the clouds. Let yourself relax, safely held by that thread as it supports your posture. From now on, this robust demeanor of yours would emanate confidence and would become habitual to you over the course of time.

2. Now imagine a moment where you felt extremely confident. Fully return to that memory now - not as an observer, but as a participant - as if you are there now, as if it is happening to you. See what you saw - hear what you heard - feel how confident and how good you felt about yourself.

3. As you continue to run through that memory in your mind, make the visuals much clearer, by making the pictures larger, the colors brighter and richer, and the sounds louder and clearer, so that you intensify your feelings.

4. Identify where in your body that feeling of confidence strikes the most. Associate a color to this feeling of confidence, let it expand all the way up from your head to the bottom of your feet. Quadruple the richness of colors as you do so.

5. Repeat that process at least four times, with the same memory or change it with a new one every time. Vividly experience that feeling of confidence spreading across your body.

The Confidence Button

I'm sure that you might be feeling great after doing the previous exercise. Let's channelize the energy and take it to the next level discovering the methodology of creating a button that you can use to trigger the sensation of confidence whenever you need it.

You might have observed that when you go out to any eatery or a pizza shop, you're greeted with the familiar smell of pizza fresh out of the oven. Chances are that you might already start salivating, even before you take your first bite!

This is an example of Classical conditioning or Pavlovian conditioning which is named after a Russian scientist called Ivan Pavlov, who conducted a series of experiments towards the start of the 20th century.

In one such experiment he did something interesting - whenever he used to give food to his dogs, he used to ring a bell at that very instant. After doing this for a while, he noticed that he had created an association between the bell and the food, as his dogs started to salivate whenever he rang the bell. On the surface it may seem that there's no reasonable linkage between the two activities, but if we rationalize our approach to this experiment and with what Pavlov concluded, we would find out that through constant repetition of any action, the neurological connections related to it in any living being strengthen up.

The very fundamental scientific reason behind this is that our brain comprises a huge number of neural pathways, where each idea or piece of information goes along its own path. Our habit formation is dependent on training our brain to create new neural pathways, where whenever we do something for the first time, a new neural pathway gets created. This helps us to re-go through that experience again more swiftly, just like when you walk down a path through a field it becomes clearer.

Studies have shown that through constant repetition of a particular behavior, its associated neural pathways increase in size. That's why most of the folks out there get 'used to' a certain kind of activity like excessive smartphone usage or substance abuse. But if we look on the bright side, the same mechanism of our brain can be used to our advantage, which leads us to our success and fulfillment by establishing a link between the brain and body through 'a button' that triggers a desired state of mind.

I recall a moment where I felt like a bundle of nerves, when I was about to take a workshop at one of the prominent convention centers in the country. Just a day before the start of the workshop, while doing all the checks and rehearsals I became a bit skeptical about everything. And the thought that this was the very first time I was on such a massive platform kept boggling me every now and then. All that I knew was that I had to give my best shot at it and for that to happen, I would require a strong sense of confidence and an imagination that showcases the workshop being conducted swiftly.

So, in order to get into that state, I did an exercise which ultimately made me steal the show. The response received on how I and the entire crew impeccably conducted the workshop was really overwhelming.

I would like to share with you exactly what I did and how you can use it to your advantage as well. In order to start things off, you'd have to keep one thing in mind- every time you feel good about anything or sense a positive flow of energy gushing down your veins, you'd have to snap your middle finger and thumb together. This would make a link which was mentioned previously, between a physical gesture and a state of confidence/optimism which you can use like a 'button' to activate the desired state of mind whenever you need it the most.

Go through the process step by step, so that you get thoroughly acquainted with it.

THE CONFIDENCE BUTTON

1. Think of an instance when you felt extremely confident. Get yourself imbued in that, see what you saw back then, listen to all the ambient sounds that were there around you. (If you aren't able think of any, just visualize how amazing it would be to have all that self-belief, confidence within you)

2. Now as you're recollecting that experience, increase the intensity of the colors, sounds and feelings that you associate with it.

3. Put your middle finger and thumb together as you intensify everything.

4. Now, snap the middle finger and thumb and rejoice the good feelings as if the moment is happening now again.

5. Repeat the aforementioned steps and replace the moment with any other beautiful memory of yours until just snapping your finger and thumb starts to give you those good vibes.

6. As you snap more often, start to ponder about any scenario where you feel you'd need to increase your confidence. Envision everything falling right in place, congruently to the way you want it to be and just relish upon it.

Doing this exercise every day would enable you to transition into the confident state more easily. Our minds are very responsive to whatever comes in their way. So, if you strengthen your imagination to feel more confident in certain scenarios, you'll realize that when they pan out in real life, you'd have automatically transitioned into that assertive state of yours.

You can simply activate that state by snapping your middle finger and thumb, thereby triggering that confidence button and focusing for a while on the feelings that start to come in, whenever you need it.

Discovering the charm in you

You must have noticed that some people simply light up the room or any area that they walk in regardless of where and when they are. This is because of the familiar term that you must have heard, that they carry a certain amount of *'charisma'* within.

Charisma is the unique characteristic of someone who possesses a personal charm and is irresistibly attractive to others. It's observed that such individuals have highly developed communication and persuasion skills that they use to influence or excite others present in the vicinity. Charisma increases a person's attractiveness, even if they don't go about it consciously. But be careful - it is not necessarily vice versa. You can meet somebody who is obviously attractive at first sight but who does not turn out to have the charisma you would expect.

One of the reasons why this happens is because charismatic people don't look out for validations or approvals from outside. They are content from within and they don't push or persuade people into liking them. I'm going to share a few tips that'll help you in developing the charm you've always wanted to have.

Becoming the charismatic version of yourself

● **Master the art of presence:** Being present in the moment is the most important aspect of charisma, with confidence being a close second. Presence is all about being truly engaged with others and paying close attention to every word that comes out of someone else's mouth. You can practice this by imagining you're watching a movie or reading a book and you're slowly learning about the main character.

● **Living with a purpose**: People with confidence and charisma also live with purpose. When you don't seem to have a mission or driving factor, you'll be confused in most of the instances. You don't need to wear your passion on your sleeve, but you need to be confident in the notion that you're alive to do something. We'll be discussing this in more depth later in upcoming chapters, but for now you can just pick a cause, a goal, a vision and ponder more about it.

● **Making conversations and channelizing it your way:** Charismatic people know how to talk to others. They can swiftly initiate a conversation, steer it in the right direction, and make others feel comfortable. Think about it, what you would and wouldn't like to talk about. If there's something that would make you feel uncomfortable, it will probably make them feel uncomfortable. It's also much easier to get a conversation going by being nice, as opposed to trying to sound brilliant.

● **A welcoming eye contact:** Sometimes a good eye contact communicates more effectively than words. Proper eye contact can express that you're listening, that you care, and that you accept the other person as an individual. Looking down or constantly shifting your gaze shows that you're uninterested and that your focus lies elsewhere. Ramit Sethi, author and founder of 'I Will Teach You to Be Rich', suggests you test the waters a little: *"try holding eye contact for a second longer than you normally would. How do you feel? How does the other person react? Remember, you have MANY opportunities to try this out. Practice with your waiter, barista, or the person at the checkout counter."*

● **Being expressive with your body:** Charismatic people express how they feel in a lot of different ways. Using your body to emphasize and enhance how you feel or what you're talking about can go a long way. Nobody thinks

59

someone who stands stiff as a board is magnetic or interesting. Above all, remember to smile. Smiling people are more approachable and more likable than someone who looks angry or uninterested.

• **Mirroring qualities:** Whenever you feel a tinge of doubt about getting into that charismatic version of yourself, you can use a mirror and while standing in front of it, you can practice all the aforementioned techniques and think about any vivid moment where you felt extremely good. Besides this, whenever you are having a conversation, you can match the other person's physical mannerisms and energy level, and you'll notice how well they'll respond to it.

You don't need to agree with everything they say or do, but merely act the way they do to some degree. This can happen naturally, depending on the social setting, but it's a simple way to increase your likability.

Just keep in mind to go through and practice these techniques every day. You have the ability to be more likable and charismatic, and the changes you need to make in the process aren't nearly as big as they may seem. Be present, confident, slowly become a master of your behavior, and watch as you start to radiate that vibe that you always wanted.

Understanding your Emotional Intelligence

Most people are familiar with general intelligence, which is an ability to learn, apply knowledge, and solve problems. But this isn't the only type of intelligence. Some people also possess an ability that they can use to tap into their emotions and use them to make their life better. This quality of understanding emotions and working along with one's feelings is known as emotional intelligence or 'emotional quotient'

Being in touch with your feelings allows you to manage stress levels and communicate effectively with other people, two skills that enhance your life both personally and professionally. Unlike Intelligence Quotient or IQ, which remains constant throughout your life, EQ can be developed and honed over time.

It's easy to put your feelings about what you experience throughout the day on the back burner. But taking time to acknowledge how you feel about experiences is essential to improving your EQ. If you ignore your feelings, you're ignoring important information that has a big effect on your mindset and the way you behave.

All the emotions you have are valid, even the negative ones. If you judge your emotions, you'll inhibit your ability to fully feel, making it more difficult to use your emotions in positive ways. Think of it this way: every emotion you have is a new piece of useful information connected to something that's happening in your world. Without this information, you'd be left in the dark about how to adequately react. That's why the ability to feel your emotions is a form of intelligence.

Openness and being agreeable go hand-in-hand when it comes to emotional intelligence. A narrow mind is generally an indication of a lower EQ. When your mind is open through understanding and internal reflection, it becomes easier to deal with conflicts in a calm and self-assured manner. You will find yourself socially aware and new possibilities will start to open up to you.

Let's take a look at some of the traits that are commonly found in emotionally intelligent people:

Self-awareness	Self-awareness is being conscious of your own feelings and motives. Emotionally intelligent people often demonstrate a high level of self-awareness. You are well acquainted with how your emotions affect you and others around you, and you don't allow your emotions to control you.
Self-regulation	People with the ability to self-regulate don't make impulsive decisions. You pause and think about the consequences of an action before proceeding.
Motivation	People with emotional intelligence are productive and driven. You think about the big picture and assess how your actions will contribute to long-term success.

| Empathy | Emotionally intelligent people are less likely to be self-centered. Instead, you empathize with others and your situations. You tend to be a good listener, slow to judge, and understanding of the needs and wants of others. For this reason, an emotionally intelligent person is often seen as a loyal, compassionate friend. |
| Social skills | It's easier for you to collaborate and work in teams. You tend to be an excellent leader because of your strong communication skills and ability to manage relationships. |

Thus, it can be rightly said that emotional intelligence plays a crucial role when establishing personal contact. We must be masters of our emotions and at the same time be able to elicit a positive response in others. As we're coming to the end of this chapter and eventually concluding our day, we'll be taking a look at one of the most crucial techniques that you'd come across in this entire book. You'll be drawing yourself off from all the negativity that might have taken a backseat within you over the years, and possibly is shaping your thoughts in a pessimistic way. Nevertheless, it's about time that we get over it and develop yet another personality trait of ours in the best way we can.

Abstinence from negativity

What comes to your mind when you hear the word – 'fasting'? I'm pretty sure that most of the people would think of it as being associated with giving up on some sort of good to eat stuff, such as a chocolate or a cake! Colloquially and in fact literally as well they are lining their thoughts correctly. But what if we broaden the spectrum a little bit and relate it with a state of mind where one takes abstinence from or 'fasts' on negativity? That's when the ideology of 'negativity fast' kicks in! Going on or practicing a 'negativity fast' means actively tuning out of the negativity around you, and reframing your mindset to a more automatic positive approach.

Many of us find it tough to quieten negativity, especially at the moment when it feels like we're faced with daunting challenges everywhere we go. Unless we make a conscious decision to step away, negativity may find ways to stick around. Therefore, it becomes essential to identify the root cause and fully work upon it to overcome any effects that it might be reflecting on the surface. A 'negativity fast' isn't about ignoring the bad things. But instead it's about making a determined effort to manage the negativity you consume, to acknowledge when you're spiraling into a cycle of unkind thoughts, and retrain your mindset.

There are a few general ways of getting started. So, discover these simple practices that you can apply to your situations, and reap the rewards of clarity and harmony.

Acknowledging negativity

The first step is to acknowledge when you're struggling with negative thoughts, or outside influences.

Therapist and coach Sean Murphy says that "by picking up on them, we welcome a state of clarity". The most useful approach to your own negative thinking is to shine a light on it. Most of our thinking is unconscious, and few people walk around intentionally trying to be negative! If you truly become aware of your thinking (your assumptions, judgments, and explanations of life), many things would become clearer. The effects of prolonged exposure to negativity can induce high anxiety. This could be a challenging friendship, an ongoing struggle with self-esteem, or social media. Understanding how the negativity you consume or even express at times, affects your mental health, is the first step to take while you are on your 'negativity fast'.

Setting an intention

Research suggests that on an average, it takes almost 66 days to form a new habit. So, you should practice the 'negativity fast' for 10 weeks, setting new habit goals such as asking yourself a question before you make a snap judgment, or dedicating a few minutes each day to note any negative conversations you have.

When you get to know about certain negative assumptions that you've made in your mind, you'll find out that they can be substituted for better thoughts quite quickly. Try changing, 'I must not make a mistake' to 'Mistakes are signs that I'm trying something new or challenging.' If I'm not making mistakes, I'm probably not making anything!

When you have set your intentions, re-read them, and then ask yourself if you've applied kindness and honesty towards them.

Manage negative influences

It's common in life to encounter someone whose energy just doesn't fit with yours, and that's perfectly alright, we are all unique. But when this clash comes at a detriment to your mental wellbeing, you can take action to distance yourself from that negative influence.

This is particularly challenging if it's someone significant in your life. But practicing meditation and mindfulness regularly can help you to observe the thoughts of frustration and negativity, without engaging with them.

With regular practice, you learn to observe and give space to your thoughts and also accept that they are just thoughts by letting them pass in their own time. This can be very difficult if your anxiety is high, but setting a small amount of time every day to practice, gets the mind in the habit of letting go of all the negativity.

Reframing your mindset

If you find yourself getting caught in a spiral of negative thoughts, it's helpful to identify the trigger, and work through that. This could be through journaling, support groups, or talking therapy.

One approach you can try is to, practice gratitude; it challenges your negative thoughts and widens your perspective. It is observed that practicing gratitude is now a research-backed method in tackling long-term feelings of negativity. It is said that gratitude is an antidote to negativity. Try it – it's very hard to be negative and thankful at the same time.

And gratitude doesn't have to exist only for the grand gestures – simplicity is the key here. A reinvigorating hot shower after a run or a favorite biscuit with a cup of tea, we need to make the time and space for those moments that we appreciate because they'll help us in feeling better and we can utilize feelings like these in countering negativity.

As you keep these points in mind, you'll start to notice the changes that happen to your cognition and eventually in your life. But to get the most optimum results, you'd have to extensively practice these techniques and would have to keep it as similar as you can to the steps mentioned. Whenever you feel low or bad about something, make sure to go through the exercises and recondition your mind thoroughly.

You'll find yourself traversing across the pool of energy that you'll harness over time and would also help others in framing their sanguine mindset. Along with it, instead of being afraid in the situations where you used to, you'd start to succeed and achieve more and eventually would break through any obstacle that comes your way.

Congratulations for stepping yourself up! Looking forward to take you to another level tomorrow as well.

Until then,

Signing off

Prriya Kaur

Some heads up for the next day: Tomorrow we're going to discover the power of a positive perspective and mindset. We're going to learn ways in which we can mold our thought process to view any scenario optimistically and become solution oriented instead of always centering our approach towards problems and not getting the desired outcomes.

"The mind is everything. What you think, you become!"

– Buddha

Day three/Step three

Positive thoughts for a Positive Life

Harnessing the power of optimistic perspectives

BEFORE STARTING OFF WITH TODAY

● **Take a while to go through the Self-image Reformulation exercise from day one.**

● **Go through this daily affirmation:**

I am born to succeed, the infinite power within me cannot fail. The divine law and order govern my life, divine peace fills my soul, and divine love saturates my mind.

Infinite intelligence guides me in all ways, God's riches flow to me freely. I am advancing, moving forward and growing mentally, spiritually, financially and in other ways.

I know these truths are sinking into my subconscious mind and will grow after their kind, today is God's Day. I chose happiness, success, prosperity and peace of mind,

All I need is within me.

● **Create a positive state of mind for the day by doing the following exercise:**

1. Think of an instance when you felt extremely confident. Get yourself imbued in that, see what you saw back then, listen to all the ambient sounds that were there around you. (If you aren't able think of any, just visualize how amazing it would be to have all that self-belief, confidence within you)

2. Now as you're recollecting that experience, increase the intensity of the colors, sounds and feelings that you associate with it.

3. Put your middle finger and thumb together as you intensify everything.

4. Now, snap the middle finger and thumb and rejoice the good feelings as if the moment happening now again.

5. As you snap more often, start to envision the rest of the day ahead and how productive it's going to be. Imagine everything falling right in place, congruently to the way you want it to be and immerse yourself in the moment by relishing upon it.

Voila! You're all set and good to go for an amazing day ahead.

A long time ago, there was a master who used to train martial arts to anyone willing to learn the craft in his vicinity. One day as he was watching a practice session in the courtyard, he came across a young fellow who was getting frustrated but wasn't able to express his feelings. He realized that the presence of other students was interfering with the young man's attempts to perfect his technique.

The master could sense the young man's frustration. He went up to the young man and tapped him on his shoulder.

"What's the problem?" he inquired.

"I don't know", said the youth, with a strained expression.

"No matter how much I try; I am unable to execute the moves properly".

"Before you can master technique, you must understand harmony. Come with me, I will explain", replied the master.

The teacher and student left the building and walked some distance into the woods until they came upon a stream. The master stood silently on the bank for several moments. Then he spoke.

"Look at the stream," he said. "There are rocks in its way. Does it slam into them out of frustration? It simply flows over and around them and moves on! Be like the water and you will know what harmony is."

The young man took the master's advice to heart. Soon, he was barely noticing the other students around him. Nothing could come in his way of executing the most perfect moves.

Throughout the course of my journey, I have come across hundreds of thousands of people. And from all the different categories that they are put into, if we consider two such categories broadly - one comprising of the people who are living their dream life, and the other one consisting of the ones who are just dragging their feet off from work to home and so forth, we'd find out that out of numerous benchmarks that are dictating this categorization, one of the most prominent ones is based upon the kind of perspective that they have.

There's an interesting story about Harry Houdini, the famous Hungarian-American illusionist of the 20th century. He was very well known for his acts and especially for the escapes that he did from extremely complex situations. In his acts he was usually completely locked up and it seemed like a next to impossible task for a common man to break through all the chains and cuffs that were put onto him. One day he announced an open challenge – that he can break free from any prison cell with top notch security. This challenge was accepted by a jail and there he was, ready full of confidence and joy, stating that he would be out of there in no time.

The day of the act finally came and there he was, all set and ready for the show with his street clothes on. He entered the jail cell and the gate was closed in front of him. He pulled out a metal piece from his belt and started to fiddle with the key hole of the lock welded in the gate. Time passed by, he kept on trying and within a few minutes the confident expression on his face started to fade away. He wasn't able to figure out how to unlock it and eventually within a matter of a couple of hours he collapsed. After a while he stood up and with just a decent amount of force, he pulled the gate sideways. He was shocked to see that the gate moved and realized that it was never locked in the first place! This was a massive learning incident for him that made him question the way he perceived things and what sort of perspective he had. The door was indeed locked, not literally, but more intensively in his mind. He gave up trying all the complex solutions whereas it was actually very simple, he just had to sway the gate open in the opposite direction.

What we can draw from this amazing example is that our perspectives, the way we look at things can actually impact the outcome of certain scenarios or situations that we come face to face with. Whether to think sensibly and work discerningly upon the challenges that come across or to feel bad, confused and crib about what's happening with one at any particular moment, the choice is entirely ours. In this chapter or Day 3, we're going to learn about orienting our minds towards a positive perspective so that we make the best out of any situation and achieve the desired result through practicing certain techniques. First let's identify your current mindset and approach towards tackling things.

Being problem-oriented vs finding solutions

As we study the mannerisms of various kinds of people, we tend to find out that given an abstract real-life problem which they can encounter in day-to-day life, the response to it can be segregated in two categories. In one category, the responses would seem a bit hay-wired and it is quite likely that out of a bunch of solutions provided (if any in the first place), most of them won't be relevant or wouldn't solve the problem entirely. Rather, even if the problem or the challenge is overcome eventually, the solution may not satisfy the one who implements it.

However, if we take a look at the responses or suggested resolutions in the second category, we'd find out a sense of absolute clarity being reflected from the solutions and they would be solving the problems or challenges to their entirety. The people who devised these solutions followed a simple but highly practical plan and it's quite likely that they were also satisfied with the outcomes that came.

These people are in no sense different from you. They might've had the same problems and difficulties that you have, but they found a formula which helped them to get the right answers to the difficult questions they faced. This same formula when applied by you can get similar results. You must have come across this familiar saying, '*It all boils down to one's perspective*'. We'd have to get ourselves fully well-versed with this, that most of us have a deep desire to understand and be understood. But this world, at times without a correct perspective, can become a very confusing place.

Well, whatever the case might be, it actually isn't that bewildering altogether if our vision is set to steer through its clarity. In fact, if we choose to see the secret power a positive perspective holds, we can set ourselves free from a world of hurt, pain, struggle and bondage. Just like your best friend or fondest family member, positivity - supports you, encourages you, lifts you to new heights, makes you feel loved even when you're alone, makes you smile, makes you laugh, gives you good luck, helps you when you're feeling blue, brings you more abundance, helps you achieve your next goal and enables us to do so much more with our life as a whole.

How do great leaders approach and tackle their challenges?

It usually happens in a typical corporate scenario that employees expect leaders to solve problems both big and small. Let's see and draw parallel conclusions on how they go about a solution-oriented approach for resolving problems.

A leader's attention is usually focused on issues of significance (financial crises, unexpected mergers, and acquisitions), which means medium-sized problems are often put aside, to return later with a vengeance! As Nobel Peace Prize winner and former US Secretary of State Henry Kissinger said, *"All too frequently a problem evaded, is a crisis invited"*.

Great leaders don't play the blame game. Instead, they use a "solution-oriented" approach to resolve problems:

They use the '*why lens*'. Highly respected leaders only solve problems within their control – the ones connected to their biggest why. They consider problems from a fundamental point of view.

They ask:

- Is this our problem?
- Why should we solve this problem?
- What happens if we don't?
- How would the solution contribute to accomplishing our most important goals?

Once they have answers, they explore the much-needed solutions!

I remember it was around 2013 and there were headlines in the local dailies that Royal Philips in Amsterdam noticed the lighting market was stagnating. At that point of time, CEO Frans van Houten asked those types of questions and armed with the answers, he concluded it would not make sense for Philips to continue with lighting. Thus, they shifted their focus on healthcare technology instead, and by approaching problems through the *why lens*, van Houten was able to change the direction of the company and keep it operable - a clear benefit of applying solution-oriented problem solving.

They are inspired by problems.

Without challenges, a business will lose its fire, passion, and dynamism. While many leaders perceive problems as distractions, first-class leaders embrace problems as opportunities to make breakthroughs. Leaders know that if they are unable to solve the problem, their competitors will! Eventually Pushing them out of the market.

Problem's fuel great leaders, providing opportunities to learn and grow to the next level. These stalwarts don't say, "Why me?" or "Why now?" They say, "Try me" or "Let's make the most of it." The greater the problem, the hungrier they are for a solution. Leaders like Richard Branson, Elon Musk, and Bill Gates view problems as golden opportunities to disrupt the market and revolutionize the customer experience.

They openly admit there is a problem.

Great leaders acknowledge that there is a problem, in case any arises, and simultaneously demonstrate the severity of the problem and the benefits of the solutions to their venture's stakeholders, partners, and shareholders.

By establishing an open environment, great leaders avoid creating silos. This way, a leader not only takes responsibility for making the problem transparent, they explore different dimensions of the problem, consequently benefiting from others' ideas.

They separate problems from people.

These pioneers ask questions until they understand the issue. A clear understanding of a problem delivers two-thirds of the solution. When people attribute blame, highly qualified leaders focus on the problem at hand, keeping emotions controlled. By doing so, they can approach the situation fairly and find a suitable solution.

They have a plan.

Great leaders do not guess. They identify the core of the problem, forecast scenarios, and produce backup plans before formulating and sharing with stakeholders. This creates the trust and commitment necessary for implementation. They assess actions and adjust whenever necessary. By analyzing, they focus on the easiest implementation route and work around any blocks standing in the way.

Top leaders make sure their organization stands steady when in crisis. They create a thorough problem-solving process. Great leaders avoid panic at all costs. They remain cool and retain a sense of humor. They know if they panic, their team members will lose hope and motivation.

They engage with those affected by the problem.

Those who have a stake in the problem and the relevant solution, often know the most. Solution-oriented leaders listen to the needs and concerns of all involved parties. When respected by the majority, leaders have buy-in and are able to focus on solutions. This caring attitude helps them build great relationships. When the relationship is good, people are prepared to walk that extra mile for their leaders.

Great leaders create an environment where team members can freely share their views without feeling insecure about their position. It is the leader's responsibility to guarantee freedom to speak up without fear of negative consequences.

They don't point fingers.

Great leaders know that finger pointing does not solve problems. It only adds new ones. It makes employees singled out, feel broken, guilty, and belittled. Instead of blaming anyone, the leader start problem solving by narrowing down the issue. When the problem has been addressed, and potentially solved, they ask their team members what they learned from the experience and how they can improve vulnerable areas.

As we read the strategic qualities that make up a 'solution-oriented' mind, now examine how you approach problems. What are the things that you keep in mind to tackle severe problems that you encounter at instances? What can you take away from the above to ensure your future approach to problem solving is more solution-oriented?

Failure: Moving you a step closer to success

As an infant, you learned how to walk by trial and error. The first time you made the effort, you fell down and returned to crawling. You ignored your fears about falling and the results you had produced. You stood up again and fell again. Eventually you stood with a wobble and fell once again.

Finally, you walked upright. Suppose as infants we had learned to fear failure. Many of us would still be crawling around on all fours.

It is the same with everything in life. Our nature is to act and produce results without fear. Yet, because we have been educated to think critically and judgmentally, we imagine strong reasons for inaction and then allow it to become our reality, even before we make an attempt. Our fear is supported by an illusion that it is possible to fail, and that failure means we are worthless.

The reality is that there is no such thing as failure. Whenever we attempt to do something and fail, we end up doing something else.

You cannot fail, you can only produce results!

Rather than judging some result as a failure, ask - "What have I learned about *what doesn't work to make it happen*?", "Can this explain something that I didn't set out to explain?", "What can I do with these results?", and "What have I discovered that I didn't set out to discover?"

Failure as your best friend

It is a paradox of life that you have to learn to fail in order to succeed. Henry Ford's first two automobile companies failed. What he learnt from his failures led him to be the first to apply assembly line manufacturing to the production of affordable automobiles in the world. He became one of the three most famous and richest men in the world during his time.

When Thomas Edison was seeking to invent the electric light bulb, he had thousands of failures. He would record the results, make adjustments and try again. It took him approximately 10,000 experiments to invent the perfect set-up for the electric light bulb. Once an assistant asked him why he persisted after so many failures. Edison responded by saying he had not failed once. He had learned 10,000 things that didn't work. There was no such thing as a failure in Edison's mind.

When you try something and produce a result which did not turn out to be what you intended, but you found that to be interesting, drop everything else and study it. B. F. Skinner emphasized this as the first principle of scientific methodology. This is what William Shockley and a multi-discipline Bell labs team did. They were formed to invent the MOS transistor and ended up instead with the junction transistor and the new science of semiconductor physics. These developments eventually led to the MOS transistor and then to the integrated circuit and to new breakthroughs in electronics and computers. William Shockley described it as a process of *'creative failure methodology.'*

If you just look at a zero '0' you see nothing; but if you pick it up and look through it, you will see the world. It is the same with failure. If you look at something as failure, you learn nothing; but look at it as your teacher and you will learn the value of knowing what doesn't work, learning something new, and the joy of discovering the unexpected.

I've mentioned this quite on and off that every action has a reaction. It is only a matter of not judging yourself as a failure but rather as someone who's committed to continuing to improve, learning, analyzing and adapting because you're choosing to believe you will ultimately reach your goals. Setbacks and learning curves are not failures. You are not a failure just because you didn't get the result you were looking for.

When I first started off with my ventures, I was faced with a lot of unknowns. I didn't have a degree in business or marketing and no one in my family was an entrepreneur and obviously I didn't produce a 6-figure income overnight. There were a lot of things I had to learn and could only learn by going through the process. It takes being willing to adjust and adapt to gain success. It also takes exploiting your strengths and finding and working within your personal unfair advantage. Every single aspect of building and growing what you're looking forward to, comes with a lot of learning curves.

That's what motivates me to share all the information I do with you. To eliminate some of that for you so you can actualize your dream faster. Challenges will still be there; you will take actions without knowing all of the answers and things won't always work the way you thought. But whatever it might be, you'd have to keep going!

Adaptability and Flexibility

There are many of us who really don't like change and we certainly don't like to have our plans or our routines interrupted. It can even make us feel somehow insecure when the things we are used to doing or the way we are used to doing them suddenly change. And then to top it, there is our personality or our temperament. Some of us may be more rigid than others or don't deal well with conflicting or "messy" personalities at work or school. Some of us panic if things change too much in our environment. Others prefer to crawl into their "cave" rather than have to deal with difficult situations.

The question to ask ourselves here is, how flexible are we in our day to day lives? That may be easy for some of us to ponder about or rather a really boggling question for others to answer. Whatever the case is, at least we can take a moment to appreciate that day by day and constantly, we're giving time to ourselves and analyzing our personalities. Now coming back to the question, how we perceive ourselves is not necessarily how others perceive us. Maybe we think we are flexible, open-minded and adventurous, but those around us might not share that opinion. Let's break down the perplexing question into several parts, consider these far from exhaustive mini-versions of it:

- How do you handle adversity?
- Do people consider you easy to work with?
- Are you open to other (different and opposing) opinions?
- Do others consider you to be flexible and adaptable?
- Are you approachable?
- Do others consider you to be open-minded?

On a scale of 1 to 10 (for each one), how would you rate your flexibility? By definition, being flexible means being able to bend without breaking. In our relationships, that is certainly true; if we don't "bend" a little, something will break, usually the relationship.

Flexibility is the key to stability

– John Wooden

The **Importance** of Being Flexible

There are a number of benefitting outcomes of instilling adaptability and flexibility in your life. As you go through each, try to imagine what sort of an impact it would make in any real-life scenario, that you believe would require you to be highly flexible.

1. It increases the trust that others have in us.

When we are able to adapt to new situations or changing circumstances, it is reassuring to others that we are able to flow with the change and not be stressed out in a panic. Others will see us as a stable ship that is not tossed every other way by the changing winds. They will put more trust in someone they can count on to be present and stable no matter what happens.

2. More personal and professional recognition for our flexibility.

Adaptability (another word for flexibility) is a tremendous asset in the business world and just about anywhere. People who tend to take things in stride receive more respect and recognition from others, simply because they admire and value the quality of being able to adapt. Furthermore, people appreciate the thoughtfulness of someone who is willing to yield and help others in a pinch rather than remaining focused on their own wants and needs.

3. It helps us to adapt to the ups and downs of change more easily.

Being a flexible or an adaptable person helps us to take life's messiness with a grain of salt. With this skill or trait, we are not bound by our perceptions or thoughts, but we can adjust the way we think and change our expectations accordingly. The ups and downs of life or the hills and valleys will not have as much of a devastating impact on us because we'd accept things and move forward.

4. It gives an opportunity for growth (We learn from adapting).

Having a flexible approach to life can teach us many things. When we are open-minded and willing to learn, we gain new understanding and open the doors to new opportunities that may have been closed if we remained rigid in inflexibility (stuck in our ways). The more we learn, the more we grow and the more we grow, the more adaptable we become.

5. We become better at taking initiative.

Being an adaptable person also means that we are more likely to take risks and open up conversations. We are more willing to try and more willing to fail. It becomes a lifestyle eventually because by taking initiatives and risks, we become more confident and empowered. It is liberating and exciting. Being a flexible person willing to try new things sets us free from being locked into the same old persona of ourselves.

6. We develop an increased capacity for creativity.

Increased creativity goes right along with a flexible mindset. A flexible person is not held down by "the way we have always done things" and is open to new ideas and creating new ways of doing things. More and more organizations are seeking out people who are creative and willing to explore new possibilities.

7. We develop more confidence in ourselves and our abilities.

As stated earlier, having a flexible mindset can help us be more confident in ourselves and our abilities. This confidence comes from being willing to let go of our routines and step out of our comfort zone to explore new zones. The more we are willing to try and fail, the more we will develop our confidence.

"Problems disappear when we are willing to become flexible."

– Roxana Jones

The **Who** and the What

Problems most often involve people and we are stuck with this fact whether we like it or not. And conflicts are usually the result of one or more individuals (or groups) being unwilling to budge on a matter. Since *'people'* are usually involved and we are a part of the lot too, maybe we should look to see what we may need to change or see things differently altogether. In any situation, there are questions we need to ask:

Who is involved and what is important? Are we looking at the person or the situation? Who is directly or indirectly involved with our choices, attitudes, and behavior? In every situation, who is being served: family members, customers, colleagues? Weighing in on who will be impacted helps us to have a perspective.

The second question to ask is *'What'*. What is happening? What is going on? Now that we have figured out how to deal with the *"people"* part of the situation, we need to deal with the nature of the problem.

What is the real situation? Is it urgent or important or both? Setting priorities can help us decide when to put our foot down and when to let it go. Are there creative options that can involve others and help them feel that they have a say? It's best to evaluate the situation and decide what is important.

In every situation, there is a goal, whether we are aware of it or not. Sometimes people may have a different perspective on the goal or different goals altogether. So, really, this step is about establishing what the common goal is -what are our long term aims? What are we looking to preserve, strengthen, improve or grow? When we put anything or anyone into a long-term perspective, it becomes easier to be less concerned with holding our position or hanging onto routine or tradition. We can let go of all our worries and just flow.

The Takeaway

We can certainly be overly flexible and this can have a negative impact around us on the opposite side of the spectrum. Simply put, when there is too much flexibility, things don't get done, expectations don't get met, people lose trust and confidence and directions are lost. Ultimately, people get annoyed, frustrated and even hurt by too much adapting and compromising.

Flexibility is a fine line. When do we flex and when do we just grip it tight, we need to set limits, have boundaries and some semblance of structure and direction. Then, once these are in place, we can use our judgment as to when to bend and when to hold tight.

Flexibility is really a non-negotiability in today's world. Everything changes and will continue to change. And we can't always expect that everything will fall into our neatly packaged way of how things should be done. Flexibility is, at its core, a survival skill - we cannot get along in life without it. If we do not develop this skill, we will fall prey to the winds of life and be a victim of change and adversity.

The new Belief system

As human beings, we are complex creatures and, in our lives, over a period of time we develop many beliefs. Some serve us, but the most limit us.

How beliefs shape your life

You make decisions every day, consciously and subconsciously. Decisions at home, at work, out in public, small, big, important, not so important, trivial, proactive and reactive decisions, you are taking them all the time.

These decisions are based on choices you make. From the kind of food, you want to eat to the dress you wish to wear, music you want to listen to, programs you want to watch, places you want to go to, people you want to meet, people you don't want to meet, goals you wish to pursue, goals that you give up on, actions you plan to take, actions you will postpone, Choices and more choices.

Do you agree?

Now these choices are based on how you feel at that moment, it could be a feeling of being happy, charged up, excited, maybe calm and inner peace or it could be something not so pleasant, like sadness, hurt, anger, guilt or shame. No matter what the feeling is, it has an impact on your choice.

Feelings are driven by your thoughts. You think a certain thought, positive or negative, inspiring or demotivating, bright, happy thoughts or thoughts of despair and fear and they in turn create the appropriate feeling within you.

Now you might be wondering as to where do these thoughts come from? Your thoughts are a result of your attitude in life. Your general outlook, your view of the world, how you approach each and every day. A good attitude will mean you are mostly filled with empowering, positive and encouraging thoughts while a poor outlook or attitude in life will see you struggling with negativity, despair, disillusionment…

And what do you think shapes your attitude in life?

…. your beliefs

Yes, your underlying beliefs shape your attitude which in turn determine your thoughts and those thoughts create feelings that drive you to make choices leading to decisions which get you the results you currently have.

What are beliefs?

Your belief system is your code, it's an agreement with yourself, as author, Don Miguel Ruiz puts it in his wonderful book 'The Four Agreements', it's the process of domestication which continues even when you grow up. Beliefs are powerful. They are you and yet you may never recognize them.

You may have heard or read about the iceberg theory. Your actions and behavior are like the visible portion of an Iceberg floating on the surface. Your underlying beliefs are like the large, invisible portion that is submerged below. You don't see it; however, it exists just the same and impacts you.

The quick-fix syndrome

Have you ever tried hard to change your thinking and not had much success? Have you been told to think positive, and it did nothing to improve your life?

This is mostly likely because you have been trying to fix the wrong element. You must first become aware of your unwanted behavior and the beliefs driving that behavior, next you must work to replace the limiting ones. Doing so will help you develop a healthier, positive attitude which in turn improves the quality of your thinking.

Start by changing your behavior and the beliefs behind it, not your thinking.

Why do you need beliefs?

They are powerful, they are your reality. They give a sense of meaning to everything around you. They are your map to this world. Without them you would be lost, unable to recognize, judge, accept, and adopt anything.

Your beliefs shape your behavior and actions, they can inspire you, pull you down, make you grow or even limit you.

In my sessions, one of the first things I ask my clients is what's working in their life, they usually begin by mentioning couple of positive developments and then unknowingly drift into narrating everything that's not ok - how they are failing, what they feel is lacking in them, how they can't seem to do anything right etc.

After a few minutes when gently reminded of the actual question, they come back on track, share more wonderful things and then slip back yet again into talking about what they feel they don't deserve, how they will be laughed at, why they will not achieve something ….

These are probably underlying beliefs speaking. These are a lifetime of negative mind chatter, conditioning coming to the fore.

This is not who they are. This is who they believe they are.

If some of your behaviors, actions are in contrast to your conscious thinking, it's probably because there are some strong beliefs driving them and you may be committed to those more than you are to the ones you wish to have. Becoming aware is an important step in working towards achieving your goals.

Some Common Beliefs

Dr. Lee Pulos, in his insightful book 'The Biology of empowerment' says we acquire most of our beliefs between the ages of 2 and 12 years as we are highly suggestible then. Your beliefs come to you from your parents, your teachers and your culture.

Let's look at some common beliefs that exist in our society:
1. You must work hard to succeed
2. Money does not come easy
3. The world is a tough place
4. Never trust strangers
5. Good people finish last

And here are five limiting ones that you might have:
1. I am not good enough
2. I will be laughed at
3. I don't deserve it
4. I will look foolish
5. What if I fail?

Beliefs by themselves do not hold you back, it's your unwillingness to change that stops you from living to your true potential.

Replacing limiting beliefs

Having looked at what beliefs are and how they impact you, it's important to understand the process of replacing the limiting ones.

Changing your beliefs is not always simple, easy or quick. Deep rooted ones need time and effort to be let go, as initially you may not even be able to recognize or identify them. A lifetime of conditioning sometimes makes it difficult to switch from one to another, even if you know the new one is better for you.

Awareness is key to achieve anything in life. It's an inner journey to understand who you are and what makes you succeed. Greater the level of self-awareness, the easier it will be to identify beliefs that help you grow and those that limit you.

Here are seven steps to replace beliefs that don't serve you:

1. Identify actions and behaviors that you are not happy with.

2. Become aware of beliefs that might be driving this behavior.
3. Question it, challenge it, and check if it's based on facts or just assumptions.
4. Next decide on the new actions, behaviors that you wish to have.
5. Find an empowering belief that will support these behaviors.
6. Practice the new behavior, repeat it, adopt, encourage, and internalize, live it.
7. Keep a track, check the progress, and continue to focus on the new behavior.

'An old belief is like an old shoe. We value its comfort so much that we fail to notice the hole in it.'
~ **Robert Brault**

What else can be done to help replace limiting beliefs?

Points to ponder:

What are some actions, behaviors you no longer wish to have in your life?
What beliefs, opinions could you be reinforcing by constantly repeating these behaviors?
What new behaviors would you like to have instead?
Which new strong beliefs would help you achieve these behaviors?
Who can help you?

I look forward to your valuable inputs!

Dealing with all sorts of Relationships

In our day to day lives, we happen to develop many sorts of relationships. Sometimes things seem to go all well with everyone and at instances even a small tiff with any individual can result in you both not talking to each other for ages. So, in order to avoid the latter scenario from happening frequently, we would have to understand how to deal with people and eventually master the art of developing and maintaining various kinds of relationships.

The quintessential thing to keep in mind while attempting to resonate with anyone is that you would need to view the world through their eyes, or as the Native American saying goes, *'to walk a mile in their moccasins'.*

A lot of great leaders like Nelson Mandela benefitted from the power of perspective and made them great arbitrators. Viewing a lot of possibilities from different perspectives, gave him an opportunity to understand the situations thoroughly and enhanced his ability to negotiate. It is also said that **his** movements which eventually made South Africa independent were a direct result of his flexibility to imagine seeing things from the perspective of his opponents. During the discussions over the future of the country, he understood the situation from every possible perspective, even considering himself standing over the shoulder of his negotiating partners and being in their position until he felt he almost 'knew their thoughts'.

As far as my experience goes, I've come to know one thing that if you're trying to view something from the eyes of other individuals, you'd have to realize that:

People's actions are dependent upon their desire to accomplish something or the need to stay true to their purpose.

It may seem that whatever they are up to or doing is on the completely opposite side of the spectrum to what we believe is best for us. Most of the time the intention behind their conduct is propitious. In case I happen to find myself in such a scenario, I tend to ponder about the possible intent of the other individual and what benefit I'll be getting out of it. By doing so, I'm able to resolve all the discord within me and approach the situation with an open mind.

Tips for building relationships

- Reach out to a colleague at work.

- Help someone else by volunteering.

- Have lunch or coffee with a friend.

- Ask a loved one to check in with you regularly.

- Accompany someone to the movies or a concert.

- Call or email an old friend.

- Go for a walk with a workout buddy.

- Schedule a weekly dinner date.

- Meet new people by taking a class or joining a club.

• Confide in a clergy member, teacher, or sports coach.

In case you're facing any sorts of troubles in maintaining your relations, I'd suggest going through the exercise on the next page

EASING OUT THE DIFFERENCES IN RELATIONSHIPS

1. Imagine someone with whom you find it difficult to get along. Revisit to any moment where you had a tiff and think as if that individual is right in front of you. See the exact same setting or surrounding, hear your inner voices and carefully notice your feelings. Now step out of yourself and let those feelings fade away.

2. After that, step into the shoes of that person whom you don't gel-up with. You can even think of putting on their persona just like a character in an augmented reality setting. Observe your surroundings from their perspective. Visualize yourself standing in front of you through their eyes. What might they be wondering to find themselves in a situation like this? Now levitate yourself off from that person or switch of the imaginary AR visor and allow the feelings to dissipate.

3. As you let the feelings fade away, think of someone whom you really appreciate especially in terms of their intellect – any friend of yours or some famous personality whom you admire. Slide into their persona and see through their eyes the interaction between you and the 'difficult to get along with' person. What's going to be their take on the scenario as they observe? What's their advice for you?

Now switch your observer's camera to a different angle and place it in such a manner where you can view both yourself and the person you were having trouble with in the same frame. Analyze from a layman's third person perspective.

4. At last, just thoroughly get well-versed with whatever insights you gained from different perspectives and slide back into your persona. Now whenever

you'd interact with that person in real life, try to position yourself in a receptive manner and sooth everything out gradually with them.

The secret power of an optimistic and positive perspective

The fact is, positivity is who we truly are. That's right, by nature we are all pure positive beings – with radiant, white light souls. We are all unique. But, here's the deal: it's up to us to use that power or to ignore it. Are you using it to your fullest potential right now?

Most of us could be a little more (or a lot more) conscious of our thought process as we are moving throughout the day. If right now you feel lacking or bitter in a particular area of your life, that's natural – it's your soul calling to you and letting you know that you could do better or things need to be resolved. We are meant to truly thrive on this beautiful planet and allow our souls to blossom to their fullest potential, not merely just survive and get by. Keep this in mind: *You deserve better!*

"To change ourselves effectively, we first have to change our perceptions"

- STEPHEN R. COVEY

Do you think, you have within you the power to make positive changes that will bring about the kind of difference you would like to have in your life? Yes, you have that power within you right now. When you are ready to make real positive changes, you won't let excuses set you back. Let go blaming other people, specific circumstances, health, family history, age, and environment. It comes down to something that only you can control – your thoughts, words, attitude, and actions. If you truly want to reach your goal you will go after it with your whole heart and overcome any obstacle.

You can start to change everything right now by choosing a positive perspective on any given situation as often as you can. Living a positive lifestyle doesn't happen overnight. But it can happen quickly if you stay conscious throughout the day of your thought process and your actions.

Harnessing the energy

To start harnessing the power of a positive perspective you need to maintain a positive mindset. This will allow you to begin drawing more abundance into your life, and in time, the life of your dreams. The way we are living in the 'now' comes down to how we think about things and our mental attitude towards life. We have the ability to make major positive changes by choosing the positive perspective in everything and in every moment.

It doesn't matter how much money you have, what your health is like, how many friends and family members you have, what you weigh, how you look or what size home you have, look at your life with a grateful heart and find something good to think and say about it. That is choosing the positive perspective.

For example, there could be a co-worker or a person in your circle that you don't really get along with, you may even strongly dislike that person; but when you open up your heart and mind and really look at this person you will find at least one good quality. In time, by focusing upon that one good quality of that person, more reasons to like that individual would surface. It's just how it works! You can apply this same theory to anything.

Be grateful for where you are right now and continue to anticipate the positive changes and growth that is coming from choosing the positive perspective at any moment. Living with a positive attitude is the only way to live your life to the fullest because you are constantly feeling joy. Feeling joyful brings more abundance.

In fact, joy is the key to living your life rather than simply existing. As long as you are happy with where you are, more abundance will continue to be drawn to you.

"Everything that irritates us about others can lead us to an understanding of ourselves"

– C.G JUNGJ

CHOOSING A POSITIVE PERSPECTIVE

When hardships and challenges come in our way, it is then that the positive perspective is needed the most. It may not be easy to find, but is always worth it. Most of the time, it involves forgiveness and an open mind to continue the search of goodness in your heart for loving & kinder thoughts.

I recall an excerpt from the book *'In Pursuit of Excellence',* that I feel is worth mentioning here, where several perspectives or beliefs were identified that could interfere with your capacity to perform to your potential and help you in leading a joyous life. It was laid down that:

- The belief that you must always have love and approval from all the people you find significant
- A belief that you must always prove to be thoroughly competent, adequate, and achieving
- The belief that emotional misery comes from external pressures and that you have little ability to control or change your feelings
- A belief that if something seems fearsome or threatening, you must preoccupy yourself with it and make yourself anxious about it
- The belief that your past remains all-important and that because something once strongly influenced your life, it has to keep determining your feelings and behavior today

You cannot have the love and approval of all people at all times, no matter what you do or how much you give of yourself; nor can you always be thoroughly competent at all things. None of us is, or ever will be, perfect at all things. We all screw up sometimes, and that's OK. That's being human.

We all have the capacity to change our perspectives, improve our focus, and directly influence our feelings. We are not locked into the limitations of our experiences. This ongoing capacity to change and improve is what makes life such a wonderful adventure. We all have the room to grow and to engage continually in the process of becoming the true version of ourselves.

It's important to develop confidence inside you, to know that every challenge will sculpt you and make you stronger. Picture yourself looking back on the situation with pride from where you have come and how much you have accomplished. Know that every difficulty is making you wiser and bringing you closer to your goals. See what it can do for you, not what it is doing to you. We must trust in this, because when we lose our faith, we slowly creep backwards. And, if this becomes a habit, we begin to create a series of problems and negative events.

Listening to your intuition can also often help you choose a more loving and positive perspective. You know what to listen to by observing your feelings when you think about it. Embrace the positive perspective or put your attention to something else that makes you feel joyous until you can come back to it with a clear mind and fresh eyes. With practice, you'll be feeling inspired and abundant in every area of your life. In fact, your life will feel like an everyday miracle!

Think about a positive perspective that you can add into your life today

To conclude today's lesson, I would like to put up a few points as a concrete technique to use generally in solving your problems:

1. Believe that for every problem there is a solution.

2. Keep calm. Tension blocks the flow of the power to think. Your brain cannot operate efficiently under stress. Go at your problem easy-like.

3. Don't try to force an answer. Keep your mind relaxed so that the solution will open up and become clear.

4. Assemble all the facts impartially, impersonally, and judicially.

5. List these facts on paper. This clarifies your thinking, bringing the various elements into an orderly system. You see as well as think. The problem becomes objective, not subjective!

Remember, life is not what happens to you, it's about your perspective. Choose to harness the power of a positive perspective!

Until then,

Prriya Kaur

"We are responsible for what we are, and whatever we wish ourselves to be, we have the power to make ourselves."

– Swami Vivekananda

Some heads up for the next day: *We've reached the kernel of this book, the most sought-after topic that would enable you to set your dreams and create routines to achieve them.*

Day Four/Step Four

Setting your dreams and routines

Clearly visualizing your goals and developing habits to achieve them

BEFORE STARTING OFF WITH TODAY

• **Take a while to go through the Self-image Reformulation exercise from day one.**

• **Go through this daily affirmation:** *I am born to succeed, the infinite within me cannot fail. The divine law and order govern my life, divine peace fills my soul, and divine love saturates my mind.*

Infinite intelligence guides me in all ways, God's riches flow to me freely. I am advancing, moving forward and growing mentally, spiritually, financially and in other ways.

I know these truths are sinking into my subconscious mind and will grow after their kind, today is God's Day. I chose happiness, success, prosperity and peace of mind,

All I need is within me.

Bring the potential of perspectives to use, by asking yourself the following questions:

1. What is that one thing in your life that makes you feel happy?

While thinking about it, I'm sure a smile must have come on your face. Sustain the Memory of *That Good Thing* for 20 seconds in your consciousness to release the positive neurotransmitters, and to further increase it, share it with someone. Besides that, daydream a little bit about that thing being forever with you and do some mental time travel.

2. Who or what around you gives you a feeling of love?

Once again, sustain the Memory of *That Good Thing* for 20 seconds in your consciousness to release the positive neurotransmitters, and to further increase it, share it with someone. Besides that, daydream a little bit about that thing being forever with you and do some mental time travel.

3. Who or what around you gives a sense of being fulfilled?

Sustain the Memory of *That Good Thing* for 20 seconds in your consciousness to release the positive neurotransmitters, and to further increase it, share it with someone. Besides that, daydream a little bit about that thing being forever with you and do some mental time travel.

4. What makes you feel passionate or enthusiastic?

Again, sustain the Memory of *That Good Thing* for 20 seconds in your consciousness to release the positive neurotransmitters, and to further increase it, share it with someone. Besides that, daydream a little bit about that thing being forever with you and do some mental time travel.

5. How would it feel to have all the wealth and abundance around you?

For the last time to conclude this exercise, sustain the Memory of *That Good Thing* for 20 seconds in your consciousness to release the positive neurotransmitters, and to further increase it, share it with someone. Make the images in your mind vivid, amplify the sounds and besides that, daydream a little bit about the abundance being forever with you and do some mental time travel.

Congratulations! You've yet again conditioned yourself and are good to go for an amazing day ahead.

One man decided to reach for his dream. But he didn't have enough strength to achieve it. So he turned to his mother:

– Mother, help me!

– Darling, I would be glad to help you, but I don't have it. And everything I have, I already gave to you…

He asked a wise man:

– Master, tell me, where can I get strength?

– It is said that it is on Mount Everest. But I couldn't find anything there, except the snowy winds. And when I came back, the time was irretrievably lost…

He asked the hermit:

– Holy Father, where to find the strength for realization of my dream?

– In your prayers, my son. And if your dream is false, you will understand it and find peace in your prayers…

The person asked everyone, but the only result of his searches was confusion.

– Why are you so confused? – asked an old man passing by.

– I have a dream, good man. But I don't know where to find strength for its realization. I asked everyone, but there was no one who could help me.

– No one? (A light flashed in the old man's eyes),

– Did you ask yourself?

The ins and outs of Dreaming

Why do we dream? Various answers have been given to this question in several instances. The way I look at it is, dreams are nothing but a reflection of our waking experience in a new form, influenced by thoughts, imaginations, and aspirations that are often about what we desire to attain, experience, or achieve. Dreams can be spontaneous, or they can be desires that we have nursed over a long time. They are often shaped by what we see regularly around us, the things we have heard or read about, or the things people we admire are doing. Here are some familiar examples of dreams and it's quite a possibility that you might have had one of them last night!

- Attending an Ivy League Institution
- Owning a company
- Being debt-free
- Being healthy and fit
- Travelling the world

You must have been told that you should dream big, have a vision that is bigger than you, you will go as high as your dreams etc. Indeed, a big dream is a powerful driving force and different people have different sets of them. But the very fundamental question that comes in is, how to go on a path to achieve them? And even prior to that, how to set our goals, visions and aspirations so that we can have an exact idea of where we want to be. Today we're going to focus upon just that and also work upon certain routines that help us keep going forth on our designed tracks. Besides that, we're also going to learn the differences between goals and dreams, so that we can clearly figure out what we want to do and where we want to be in a certain amount of time, say a couple of years or months down the line.

Difference between goals and dreams

Goals and dreams are two concepts that are often used interchangeably in the quest for success. Although they can be used to complement one another and can work together to facilitate success. They actually mean two different things. Let's understand the subtle yet significant differences between them.

In order to have a dream, you need to engage your thoughts and imagination. This means thinking deeply about what you want to achieve, where you want to go, and to what extent you want to achieve those things. For dreams, everything ends in the realm of imagination if nothing is done thereafter.

Unlike dreams, goals require a commitment towards achieving the desired end. This includes deciding the size of the goals, planning the order of events that will lead to achieving them, and the timeline within which they should be achieved. You can have a dream anytime, anyhow, and without any form of preparation or formality. This is not the same with goals. Goals must be set thoughtfully, and conscientiously.

They must be clearly written down and should be S.M.A.R.T – Specific, Measurable, Attainable, Realistic and Time based.

S = Specific

Be as clear and specific as possible with what you want to achieve. The narrower your goal, the more you'll understand the steps necessary to achieve it.

Example: "I want to earn a position managing a development team for a startup tech company."

M = Measurable

What evidence will prove you're making progress toward your goal? For example, if your goal is to earn a position managing a development team for a startup tech company, you might measure progress by the number of management positions you've applied for and the number of interviews you've completed. Setting milestones along the way will give you the opportunity to re-evaluate and course-correct as needed. When you achieve your milestones, remember to reward yourself in small but meaningful ways.

Example: "I will apply to three open positions for the manager of a development team at a tech startup."

A = Achievable

Have you set an achievable goal? Setting goals you can reasonably accomplish within a certain timeframe will help keep you motivated and focused. Using the above example of earning a job managing a development team, you should know the credentials, experience and skills necessary to earn a leadership position. Before you begin working towards a goal, decide whether it's something you can achieve now or whether there are additional preliminary steps you should take to become better prepared.

Example: "I will update my resume with relevant qualifications, so I can apply to three open positions for the manager of a development team at a tech startup."

R = Relevant

When setting goals for yourself, consider whether or not they are relevant. Each of your goals should align with your values and larger, long-term goals. If a goal doesn't contribute toward your broader objectives, you might rethink it. Ask yourself why the goal is important to you, how achieving it will help you and how it will contribute toward your long-term goals.

Example: "To achieve my goal of being in leadership, I will update my resume with relevant qualifications so I can apply to three open positions for the manager of a development team at a tech startup."

T = Time-based

What is your goal time-frame? An end-date can help provide motivation and help you prioritize. For example, if your goal is to earn a promotion to a more senior position, you might give yourself six months. If you haven't achieved your goal in that timeframe, take time to consider why. Your timeframe might have been unrealistic, you might have run into unexpected roadblocks or your goal might have been unachievable.

Example: "To achieve my goal of being a leader, I will update my resume with relevant qualifications so that I can apply to three open positions for the manager of a development team at a tech startup this week."

Why should I use SMART goals?

Using the SMART goal framework sets boundaries and defines the steps you'll need to take, resources necessary to get there and milestones that indicate progress along the way. With SMART goals, you're more likely to achieve your goals efficiently and effectively.

Here are a few examples of how SMART goals can benefit people in different circumstances:

Example 1

I will obtain a job as a high school math teacher within three months after graduating with my Bachelor of Science in Education.

Specific: The goal of becoming a high school math teacher is well-defined

Measurable: Success can be measured by the number of applications, interviews and job offers.

Achievable: The goal setter will have the appropriate degree for the job.

Relevant: The goal setter is planning to get a job in the education industry after getting an education degree.

Time-based: The goal setter has set a deadline to achieve his objective i.e. within three months' post-graduation.

Example 2

I will earn a promotion to senior customer service representative by completing the required training modules in three months and applying for the role at the end of next quarter.

Specific: The goal setter has clearly set the objective to be promoted as a senior customer services representative.

Measurable: Success can be measured by training module completion, filing the application and earning the promotion.

Achievable: The goal setter will complete the training necessary to earn the promotion.

Relevant: The goal setter is planning to apply for the promotion after finishing their training modules.

Time-based: The goal setter has set a deadline to achieve their objective at the end of the following business quarter

Captured Dreams Become Goals

There can be dreams without goals. Dreams can go on and on and end only in fantasy. However, when they are captured, they can become actionable goals that can, indeed materialize. There is a Yoruba proverb that can be translated thus: *"S/he who finds money in the dream and gets excited should be told to focus on working hard so as not to become a victim of poverty."* While the proverb is primarily about night dreams, it can apply to imaginative dreaming too.

To realize your dream, it must be captured and turned into a goal; then, you will have to create a strategy and follow it up with hard work. Goals are the steps you set out to take after you are convinced that your dream is truly worth it. These steps will outline what you should do and how you should do to attain your dream.

Dreams Are Free, but Goals Come with a Price.

Dreams come without costs. You can dream as many times as you want in a day without restriction. However, goals are not like that. You have to think about whether your goals are achievable or not when setting them. Because of the costs (sacrifices) associated with getting your goals done, it places a limit on which goals you can set per time. There are no structures to dreams, neither are there limits to how far you can dream. But goals have to be framed. They must be clearly defined with measurable objectives and a timeline.

You can dream to inspire yourself and aspire to a greater future, but if you want to experience real change, you have to be specific about what you want and how you want to get there. Goals are the commitments made towards creating change.

It would be apt to say that there is no goal without a dream. Dreams must come first because dreams give birth to goals. You must have a desire and nurture it in your mind until it becomes a burning desire that you are ready to pursue. That is when they can be turned to goals.

Dreaming Big

I have always been a dreamer. As far as I can remember, I had these wild fantasies and visions of doing and achieving great things in my life. But I'm not alone in that aspect. There are plenty of dreamers out there. And while our society might work to dismiss some of us as pure noise, there are enormous benefits to dreaming often, and dreaming big.
If you're a dreamer like me, then we must be kindred spirits. Dreaming involves holding tight to a vision of a better life, one with success and abundance. Getting there might be difficult, but having to deal with setbacks and failures along the way is surely worth it. Anyone who's achieved a big goal knows just how true that statement is. Some of us might like to dream, in fact we all dream differently. We don't always hold tight to those dreams, knowing that we can and will do anything in our power to make them a reality. The truth of the matter is that many of us give up on our dreams. We throw in that proverbial towel when the going gets tough. We give up rather than persist through the torment and pain of another failure. But being a starry-eyed

dreamer isn't about giving up. Dreaming often and dreaming big actually provides us with a platform for growth and success.

Children dream big. It's part of their genetic fiber - their overall make-up, they never think small because they aren't hindered by the standard limitations that hold adults back. If you ask a child what he wants for Christmas, he might say, "I want two swimming pools! One in the backyard, and one in the front." While it's easy to dismiss a child's dreams as being silly or unrealistic, who's to say that so?

Who's to say any of our dreams are silly or unrealistic? Just because something goes against the grain, or runs in the opposite direction of societal norms, it doesn't mean that it's impossible. We can all use a bit of childlike amusement in ourselves. There's absolutely nothing wrong with it. And if your dreams don't scare you, then they're not big enough.

The only thing holding you back from achieving them, is yourself. We can be our own worst enemies in so many instances, especially when we don't believe wholeheartedly in ourselves. Let us take a look at some of the points, that'll help us in dreaming big:

1. Thoughts are things, what you think, you become.

Dreamers are a select crowd. They have a unique way of envisioning things deeply enough, almost able to see them right before their very eyes. And that holds some serious power and sway. Why? Because thoughts are things. What we think, we become. Undoubtedly, you've heard the expression before, but here's why it's so powerful. Any person in history that's achieved wild results has been able to deeply envision their dreams before they became a reality. Every single person who's gone on to do something notable can attest to this. The dream precedes reality, always.

When you go to check out cars, why do you think the test drive is such a powerful selling feature? Companies know that once they get you behind the wheel, the deal is almost set and done. The act of physically driving a car and feeling what it feels like to be behind the wheel is one way to bring a dream into reality. And they know that.

Similarly, this is also why an open house or real estate tour is such a vital tool. Since all people aren't able to envision the dream of living in a particular home, seeing it firsthand helps to do that. And, when the home is ideally furnished to your standards, you're far more likely to picture yourself living there, and thus potentially see yourself buying that house. No words have been truer. If you're a dreamer, dream big and see those dreams as clearly and vividly as the light of day. Write them out in great detail.

Don't allow other people to discourage you just because your dreams are big. They should be big enough to scare you half to death. That's when you know you've got hold of something worthwhile.

2. Your focus is altered and you notice different things.

Take two people who go to the same party. One person hones in on a couple arguing in the corner, bickering endlessly. He says that the party was awful because all he saw were people arguing. Another person goes to the same party, dances, laughs, meets great new people he would call friends, and goes home, eventually telling everyone he had one of the best nights of his life.
So, what separates these two people?

Focus - Focus is everything.

What you focus on, you get more of. No matter what it is we're talking about in life, if you focus on it, you'll get more of it. When professional race car drivers are taught about steering out of trouble, they're taught vehemently about focus and where their eyes and head need to be looking. Because that's where your car will be going. If you spin out of control and you focus on the wall, worried, praying, and fearing you might hit, you'll hit it. Why? You focused on it.
Similarly, people who dream big are focused on those dreams. They live and breathe those dreams. They have wild-eyed fantasies about those dreams coming to fruition. And, if they don't give up, those dreams do come true because they have their focus on them. They steer towards them, even in the difficult times when it seems like they might just be going to crash and burn.
Of course, nothing worthwhile will ever come easy, but focus is a key reason why some big dreamers are able to achieve outlandish results. Even with all the negativity that surrounds them, they push through. But it's those lofty dreams that help them to move past the potential fear of failure and stumbling blocks along the way.
Don't be afraid to dream big, because it will alter your focus. It will help to adjust your way of thinking, to push you forward rather than hold you back. Ignore the naysayers. There will always be naysayers. Dream big and don't be afraid to chase those dreams.

3. Suddenly, your life moves in the right direction.

The subconscious mind is incredibly powerful. More so than even we've uncovered with modern science. In fact, we've only really begun to scratch the surface of our understanding of things such as the brain, the mind, and their role in human consciousness. But, without delving into a discussion about the enormity of things beyond our understanding, one thing is clear: the mind is incredibly powerful.

When you dream, you hold fast to ideas that live in your conscious mind, but also find their way into your subconscious mind. The subconscious mind aids in processing up to 60,000 thoughts per day, which is an enormous number when you stop to think about it. Those thoughts control your every moment and movement in life.

What you think fosters what you feel, and what you feel fosters how you behave, and how you behave fosters your life's experiences, and your life's experiences foster your values and your beliefs. So, those thoughts (much of which are occurring on the subconscious layer of your mind) have an enormous impact on your life.

If you want to control the direction of just where you're headed, you have to control your thoughts. When you dream big, your thoughts are steeped in abundance rather than lack. Even if, in reality, you're living in a state of absolute lack, you're broke, or you've failed over and over again, as long as you can dream big, the direction of your life, and its resultant outcome, will eventually change.

4. You begin to realize that self-improvement is a necessity, not an option.

Some dreamers know that in order to realize their dreams, they need to improve their lives. Self-improvement becomes more of a necessity and less of an option. Dreamers realize that they can't fulfill their dreams by doing the same things over and over again while expecting different results. They need to improve and move forward, rather than continue on the same path and be left behind.

But when you don't dream, and you don't envision a better life for yourself, one of abundance, you continue to live in a state of lack, immersed in bad habits and a status quo that seemingly doesn't change. In turn, when you dream, you realize the endless possibilities that might exist if you were to fulfill those dreams, which drive change.

Without changing, there's no way to fulfill our dreams, dreamers know that as a fact. But it takes a certain type of dreamer; one who can realize his or her full potential to turn dreams into reality. It isn't a brain surgery, but it does involve the consistent effort of following through day in and day out, and not giving yourself excuses. If you're a dreamer, and you've set some serious goals for yourself, then embark on a quest of self-improvement. Work on developing a set of good habits, building an empowering morning routine, and eliminating the bad habits in your life. If you want to fulfill your dreams, then it's not enough to just envision a better life; you have to actually do something about it.

5. When you fail, you can recover quicker.

I know, I know. Failure is painful. I've been there too many times. But those failures have served me rather than hindered me. I didn't realize it at the time, but those failures actually benefited me in the long run. I grew mentally, spiritually, and emotionally. I experienced physical pain, but came out metaphysically ahead. There's something about failure that does such a number on us, similar to the fact that it is impossible to see the forest through the trees when we're going through it.

When we're in the midst of that pain, we could care less about how it's going to supposedly improve our lives in the long term. But it does. And as a dreamer, you've likely failed, and you'll likely fail some more. But that's okay.

Dreamers recover from failure quicker than ordinary people. Why? Because they dream big. After the initial upset and pain wash is over, they pick themselves up and brush themselves off, and they try it again. And the really persistent dreamers keep trying it until they achieve those lofty dreams that they set for themselves, no matter what it takes.

The truth of the matter is that when you fail you tend to ponder, and when you succeed you tend to party. But failure breeds the skills that are necessary for success in the long term, and not just the short-lived kind that we can experience with momentary (but quickly fleeting) feelings of bliss. Don't be afraid to dream just because you might fail, it will help build character and give you the tools to succeed in the long term.

6. You begin to effectively manage your time.

While you might not think that dreamers are effective time managers, the ones that are serious about achieving their dreams most certainly are. If you can effectively manage your time, there's no limitations to what you can achieve. But, if you're likely to get sidetracked often, then achieving your dreams might be a little bit more arduous or strenuous.

Time management is definitely a skill that's necessary for people who are serious about their dreams. Because, even if you can vividly imagine those dreams and what your life would be like if they were to be fulfilled, turning them into a reality is far more difficult without taking constant action amidst the framework of an effective time-management system.

Time is our most precious resource. We all have the same amount of it. Just 24 hours in a day. No one gets more time than the other person, so it's essentially life's greatest equalizer. But what differs is just how we use the precious little

108

time that we have. Do we waste it away? Or, do we leverage it, efficiently using it to achieve our dreams?

That makes all the difference. If you're serious about your dreams, then you know all too well that you need a good system to manage your time. Whether you use the quadrant time management system, or you pick another one, it's entirely up to you. What does matter is that you pick something and ensure that the precious hours, minutes, and seconds in your life don't go waste.

7. The word *impossible* doesn't apply to you anymore!

As a dreamer, you ignore the word impossible. In fact, the word impossible simply says to you — I'm Possible.

Anything is possible when you can vividly dream of it.

While others might try to dissuade you from seeing those dreams come to life, you won't listen to them. You're a dreamer. You're wild-eyed. You're going to fulfill your dreams no matter what it takes. We dreamers don't look at the impediments in the road. We don't see the stumbling blocks. And we ignore our past failures. We push forward, chasing those dreams. We don't stop and we certainly don't give up. We might hit serious rough patches and fail over and over again, but we pick ourselves up and try again and again until we achieve what we set out to achieve.

That's what being a dreamer is all about. There's no such thing as impossible. Everything is possible. You can see it so clearly and vividly that you can almost taste it. And that's part of the battle. That's the beauty of being a dreamer.

8. You begin to seek out inspiration in others who've succeeded.

One of the ways dreamers fulfill their dreams is by modeling others who've come before them. When you hold a dream so vividly in your mind that it almost feels real, you look for any and every way you can make that dream into a reality. And to do that, we often turn to the people who inspire us. We look to people who've waged the battles but have won the war.

It's never easy to fulfill your dreams, but it does seem a little less overwhelming when you look at others who've achieved lofty goals even in the face of seemingly insurmountable circumstances. How did they do it? What was the process? What were they thinking? What challenges did they have to face and overcome? And just how did they pull it off?

You become like a detective, and the crime you're investigating is a success. You begin to put all the pieces together in the puzzle, and little by little, you figure it out. Looking to your inspiration in others that fulfilled their dreams who might have been in far worse circumstances initially than you were, success doesn't seem that fleeting.

"Every day is a new day to hope, dream and try again."

– Heather Wolf

9. When bad habits hold you back, you begin to notice it more.

One of the biggest things that hold us back from achieving greatness is, well, ourselves. We can be our own worst enemies. But when you're a dreamer, you begin to notice those things more. You notice the bad habits that hold you back. You recognize the patterns of limiting behavior that are keeping you from achieving your goals.

It doesn't happen right away. Nor is this an overnight process. But with failure and pain, comes understanding and growth. You begin to take notice of things that you think, say, and do because your dreams are so important to you that you realize what you do on a daily basis matters to your overall trajectory in life.

It's not easy to deal with bad habits. They take constant effort. But anyone can quit their bad habits when they want something badly enough. If your dreams are that vivid and you have strong-enough reasons why you absolutely must achieve them, you realize that you have no choice but to deal with your bad habits. Otherwise, they deal with you.

10. You start sweating the small stuff.

Dreamers sweat the small stuff. We have no choice.

You realize, as a dreamer, that the little things add up. While they don't seem like much at the moment, over time, they amount to a lot. And that either holds us back or pushes us forward. A few minutes wasted or gained here and there become important over time. A few dollars spent here or saved there begin to matter a whole lot more.

You also begin analyzing the numbers, because analytics are everything when you're chasing your dreams. If your dream is to lose weight, create a wildly-successful startup, or do just about anything else in life, you need to track your results. How else would you know just how far you've come, where you are today, and how much more work you've got left? It would be more difficult, that's for certain.

Even if, as a dreamer, you don't initially sweat the small stuff, you do so over time. You realize that it's an integral part of the process. You can't get to where

110

you're going without plotting your results and seeing what's working and what's not. When you see what isn't working, because you're sweating the small stuff, you can make changes early on. And eventually, you can fulfill those lofty dreams.

11. Little by little, your small achievements stack up.

In the beginning, the dreams feel immense. You wonder how we're ever going to achieve them. You think about the enormity of the task ahead. But, little by little, you have small wins. One achievement here and another there adds up over time. And, eventually, those wins start to stack up one by one.

This helps to build momentum, moving you closer to your goals. When you can see these things coming to pass over time, it's far more motivating to help you push just a little bit further. We improve in stages, week by week, month by month, and year by year, but we don't stop holding those dreams vividly in our minds. Every dreamer knows that their big dreams won't come easy. Otherwise, they wouldn't be worthwhile. If everyone could do it, then what would be the challenge in it? Would we still call it a dream?

No, as a dreamer, you realize that there's a long road ahead, but you're also willing to do what it takes. And, over time, you'll reach and fulfill those dreams. It doesn't happen overnight. But, eventually it happens.

Writing Your Personal Purpose Statement

Now that you've explored your purpose, I'd like you to use your answers to the questions above to create your personal purpose statement. Your personal purpose statement should be a simple sentence that expresses your values and what you want to share with others through your life's work.

Your fellow dreamers, ideal customers, future business partners, mentors, and colleagues should be able to easily remember your personal purpose statement. If I had to guess, I'd say that Richard Branson's personal purpose statement is "to build brands that allow others to experience life as an adventure." I think that the musically talented Adele's purpose statement is "to reflect the world's emotion through music" and that of Steve Jobs' personal statement was "to create a future forward world through technology." My own purpose statement is "to create a platform that allows people to activate their purpose and empower their dreams."

Now create your own purpose statement. If you need help getting started, choose five words from the purpose word bank.

Serve	teach	give	provide
Love	create	build	grow
Future	technology	innovation	develop

Use those words to craft a personal purpose statement such as, "My purpose is to provide books in rural communities," or "My purpose is to create more learning opportunities for senior citizens." Use the following space to develop your own personal purpose statement.

_____

_____

_____

_____

_____

After you develop the first draft of your personal purpose statement, invite a fellow dreamer or mentor to "interview" you with the following questions. If no one's available around you, you can use a mirror for this as well.

Do your best to answer them as fully as possible:

What did you learn from exploring your purpose?

How are you currently using these new findings in your business, company, or venture?

How does your purpose connect with your dream?

If you're not living your purpose now, what would you need to do to close the distance between your purpose and where you want to be?

After you answer these questions, ask this person or yourself for feedback, about whether your personal purpose statement matches what he or she knows about you or what you know about yourself. Also, ask to suggest ways that you can demonstrate this purpose in your everyday life. Sometimes, others are able to recognize gifts, talents, and skills that we don't see in ourselves.

Next, you'll work on clarifying your dream's purpose, which is somewhat different from your personal purpose. Again, your personal purpose is an overarching motivation that guides all the dreams you're going to develop. It's the backbone of what matters to you and what you want to contribute to the world, and we've distilled all that into a personal purpose statement.

Your dream's purpose is specific to one particular project - the goal, product, service, etc., that you're developing at the moment. It's the heart of the reason that you're going after this dream, and we're going to distill that down into a mission statement.

5 Questions to Discover Your Dream's Purpose

It's time to have a heart-to-heart conversation with your dream. Invite your idea into the room and tell it to have a seat. This idea might be a book, a new invention, a new blog, a new community, or a new movement. Speak as you would to a friend. Say, "Hey, Dream! I'm delighted that you've chosen me and am thrilled that we get to make this journey together. I know you're giving me a chance to leave a mark on the world, and I want to give you a chance to fulfill your purpose of serving others."
In this exercise, you'll speak for your goal as you answer the following five questions. Be as specific as you can. Even try to provide details of a timeline or the number of people you expect will be affected. Remember, your dream is a grand opportunity, so the more detailed is the description, the more vivid the dream will seem.

1. **Why do you want to exist?**
2. **Who will you help when you get here?**
3. **What benefits and/or possibilities will become available to others because you will exist?**
4. **What problems will be solved because you exist?**
5. **What joy will you bring to the world?**

The media and its influences on our dreams

Lifestyle changes have been increasing slowly since the introduction of media. Media - films, television shows, magazines, and more recently, the Internet (i.e., self-written blogs and popular websites) have been the main sources of lifestyle influence around the world, which quite heavily modify our ways of thinking and approach towards our dreams.

Lifestyle changes include how people eat, dress, and communicate. Lifestyle trends have usually been shaped up by the <u>wealthy</u> and <u>famous</u>, whether they are spotted at leisure or in a paid advertisement.

At the dawn of the media age, the newspaper, popular magazines, and TV allowed the general public to glimpse lifestyles that before were only available in the imagination. After its creation, the Internet became arguably the most powerful medium for spotting and influencing trends, not just by celebrities but by the average person. The computer era has changed the way people obtain their news, perspectives and communication and with the advent of the Android phone and its relative ease of uploading photos to various social media sites, one can get an idea of how quickly an idea, review, or coveted object can be shared.

Douglas Keller, a well-known American Academic writes,

"Radio, television, film, and the other products of media culture provide materials out of which we forge our very identities; our sense of selfhood; our notion of what it means to be male or female; our sense of class, of ethnicity and race, of nationality, of sexuality; and of 'us' and 'them'".

The Stressful ambience all around

In today's fast-paced world, it's quite likely that you must have heard or experienced yourself, something that we call Stress. Stress is your body's way of responding to any kind of demand or threat. When you sense danger, whether it's real or imagined, the body's defenses kick into high gear in a rapid, automated process known as the "fight-or-flight" reaction or the "stress response."

The stress response is the body's way of protecting you. When working properly, it helps you stay focused, energetic, and alert. In emergency situations, stress can save your life by giving you extra strength to defend yourself, for example, spurring you to slam on the brakes to avoid a car accident.

Stress can also help you rise to meet challenges. It's what keeps you on your toes during a presentation at work, sharpens your concentration when you're attempting the game-winning free throw, or drives you to study for an exam when you'd rather be watching TV. But beyond a certain point, stress stops being helpful and starts causing major damage to your health, mood, productivity, relationships, and your quality of life.

If you frequently find yourself feeling frazzled and overwhelmed, it's time to take action to bring your nervous system back into balance. You can protect yourself and improve how you think and feel by learning how to recognize the signs and symptoms of chronic stress and taking steps to reduce its harmful effects.

Fight-or-flight response: what happens in the body?

When you feel threatened, your nervous system responds by releasing a flood of stress hormones, and including adrenaline and cortisol, which rouse the body for emergency action. Your heart pounds faster, muscles tighten, blood pressure rises, breath quickens, and your senses become sharper. These physical changes increase your strength and stamina, speed up your reaction time, and enhance your focus preparing you to either fight or flee from the danger at hand.

Your nervous system isn't very good at distinguishing between emotional and physical threats. If you're super stressed over an argument with a friend, a work deadline, or a mountain of bills, your body can react just as strongly as if you're facing a true life-or-death situation. And the more your emergency stress system is activated, the easier it becomes to trigger, making it harder to shut off.

If you tend to get stressed out frequently, like many of us in today's demanding world, your body may exist in a heightened state of stress most of the time. And that can lead to serious health problems. Chronic stress disrupts nearly every system in your body. It can suppress your immune system, upset your digestive and reproductive systems, increase the risk of heart attack and stroke, and speed up the aging process. It can even rewire the brain, leaving you more vulnerable to anxiety, depression, and other mental health problems.

The most dangerous thing about stress is how easily it can creep up on you. You get used to it. It starts to feel familiar, even normal. You don't notice how much it's affecting you, even as it takes a heavy toll. That's why it's important to be aware of the common warning signs and symptoms of stress overload.

What causes stress?

The situations and pressures that trigger stress are known as stressors. We usually think of stressors as being negative, such as an exhausting work schedule or a rocky relationship. However, anything that puts high demands on you can be stressful. This includes positive events such as getting married, buying a house, going to college, or receiving a promotion.

Of course, not all stress is caused by external factors. Stress can also be internal or self-generated, when you worry excessively about something that may or may not happen, or have irrational, pessimistic thoughts about life.

Finally, what causes stress depends, at least in part, on your perception of it. Something that's stressful to you may not faze someone else; they may even enjoy it. While some of us are terrified of getting up in front of people to perform or speak, others live for the spotlight. Where one person thrives under pressure and performs best in the face of a tight deadline, another will shut down when work demands escalate. And while you may enjoy helping to care for your elderly parents, your siblings may find the demands of caretaking overwhelming and stressful.

Whatever event or situation is stressing you out, there are ways of coping with the problem and regaining your balance. Some of life's most common sources of stress include:

Stress at work

While some workplace stress is normal, excessive stress can interfere with your productivity and performance, impact your physical and emotional health, and affect your relationships and home life. It can even determine the difference between success and failure on the job. Whatever your ambitions or work demands, there are steps you can take to protect yourself from the damaging effects of stress, improve your job satisfaction, and bolster your well-being in and out of the workplace.

Job loss and unemployment stress

Losing a job is one of life's most stressful experiences. It's normal to feel angry, hurt, or depressed, grieve for all that you've lost, or feel anxious about what the future holds. Job loss and unemployment involves a lot of change all at once, which can rock your sense of purpose and self-esteem. While the stress can seem overwhelming, there are many steps you can take to come out of this difficult period stronger, more resilient, and with a renewed sense of purpose.

Financial stress

Many of us, from all over the world and from all walks of life, are having to deal with financial stress and uncertainty at this difficult time. Whether your problems stem from loss of work, escalating debt, unexpected expenses, or a combination of factors, financial worry is one of the most common stressors in modern life. But there are ways to get through these tough economic times, ease stress and anxiety, and regain control of your finances.

Caregiver stress

The demands of caregiving can be overwhelming, especially if you feel that they are over your head or you have little control over the situation. If the stress of caregiving is left unchecked, it can take a toll on your health, relationships, and state of mind, eventually leading to a burnout. However, there are plenty of things you can do to rein in the stress of caregiving and regain a sense of balance, joy, and hope in your life.

Grief and loss

Coping with the loss of someone or something you love is one of life's biggest stressors. Often, the pain and stress of loss can feel overwhelming. You may experience all kinds of difficult and unexpected emotions, from shock or anger to disbelief, guilt, and profound sadness. While there is no right or wrong way to grieve, there are healthy ways to cope with the pain that, in time, can ease your sadness and help you come to terms with your loss, find new meaning, and move on with your life.

How much stress is too much?

Because of the widespread damage stress can cause, it's important for you to know your own limit. But just how much stress is "too much" differs from person to person. Some people seem to be able to roll with life's punches, while others tend to crumble in the face of small obstacles or frustrations. Some people even thrive on the excitement of a high-stress lifestyle.

Factors that influence your stress tolerance level include:

Your support networks.

A strong network of supportive friends and family members is an enormous buffer against stress. When you have people you can count on, life's pressures don't seem as overwhelming. On the flip side, the lonelier and more isolated you are, the greater your risk of succumbing to stress.

Your sense of control.

If you have confidence in yourself and your ability to influence events and persevere through challenges, it's easier to take stress in stride. On the other hand, if you believe that you have little control over your life, that you're at the mercy of your environment and circumstances, stress is more likely to knock you off course.

Your attitude and outlook.

The way you look at life and its inevitable challenges makes a huge difference in your ability to handle stress. If you're generally hopeful and optimistic, you'll be less vulnerable. Stress-hardy people tend to embrace challenges, have a stronger sense of humor, believe in a higher purpose, and accept change as an inevitable part of life.

Your ability to deal with your emotions.

If you don't know how to calm and soothe yourself when you're feeling sad, angry, or troubled, you're more likely to become stressed and agitated. Having the ability to identify and deal appropriately with your emotions can increase your tolerance to stress and help you bounce back from adversity.

Your knowledge and preparation.

The more you know about a stressful situation, including how long it will last and what to expect, the easier it is to cope. For example, if you go into surgery with a realistic picture of what to expect post-operation, a painful recovery will be less stressful than, if you were expecting to bounce back immediately.

The Tension management

If you're living with high levels of stress, you're putting your entire well-being at risk. Stress wreaks havoc on your emotional equilibrium, as well as your physical health. It narrows your ability to think clearly, function effectively, and enjoy life. It may seem like there's nothing you can do about stress. The bills won't stop coming, there will never be more hours in the day, and your work and family responsibilities will always be demanding. But you have a lot more control than you might think.

Effective stress management helps you break the hold stress has on your life, so you can be happier, healthier, and more productive. The ultimate goal is a balanced life, with time for work, relationships, relaxation, and fun, the resilience to hold up under pressure and meet challenges head on. But stress management is not one-size-fits-all. That's why it's important to experiment and find out what works best for you. The following stress management tips can help you do that.

Tip 1: Identify the sources of stress in your life

Stress management starts with identifying the sources of stress in your life. This isn't as straightforward as it sounds. While it's easy to identify major stressors such as changing jobs, moving, or going through a divorce, pinpointing the sources of chronic stress can be more complicated. It's all too easy to overlook how your own thoughts, feelings, and behaviors contribute to your everyday stress levels. Surely, you may know that you're constantly worried about work deadlines, but maybe it's your procrastination, rather than the actual job demands, that is causing the stress.

To identify your true sources of stress, look closely at your habits, attitude, and excuses:

- Do you explain away stress as temporary ("I just have a million things going on right now") even though you can't remember the last time you took a breather?
- Do you define stress as an integral part of your work or home life ("Things are always crazy around here") or as a part of your personality ("I have a lot of nervous energy, that's all")?
- Do you blame your stress on other people or outside events, or view it as entirely normal and unexceptional?

Until you accept responsibility for the role you play in creating or maintaining it, your stress level will remain outside your control.

Start a stress journal

A stress journal can help you identify the regular stressors in your life and the way you deal with them. Each time you feel stressed, keep track of it in your journal or use a stress tracker on your phone. Keeping a daily log will enable you to see patterns and common themes. Write down:

- What caused your stress (make a guess if you're unsure)?

- How you felt, both physically and emotionally.

- How you acted in response.

- What you did to make yourself feel better.

Tip 2: Practice the 4 A's of stress management

While stress is an automatic response from your nervous system, some stressors arise at predictable times e.g. your commute to work, a meeting with your boss or a family gathering. When handling such predictable stressors, you can either change the situation or change your reaction.

When deciding which option to choose in any given scenario, it's helpful to think of the *four A's: avoid, alter, adapt, or accept.*

The four A's – Avoid, Alter, Adapt & Accept

Avoid unnecessary stress

It's not healthy to avoid a stressful situation that needs to be addressed, but you may be surprised by the number of stressors in your life that you can eliminate.

Learn how to say "no." Know your limits and stick to them. Whether in your personal or professional life, taking on more than you can handle is a surefire recipe for stress. Distinguish between the "should" and the "musts" and, when possible, say "no" to take on too much.

Avoid people who stress you out. If someone consistently causes stress in your life, limit the amount of time you spend with that person, or end the relationship.

Take control of your environment. If the evening news makes you anxious, turn off the TV. If traffic makes you tense, take a longer but less-traveled route. If going to the market is an unpleasant chore, do your grocery shopping online.

Pare down your to-do list. Analyze your schedule, responsibilities, and daily tasks. If you've got too much on your plate, drop tasks that aren't truly necessary to the bottom of the list or eliminate them entirely.

Alter the situation

If you can't avoid a stressful situation, try to alter it. Often, this involves changing the way you communicate and operate in your daily life.

Express your feelings instead of bottling them up. If something or someone is bothering you, be more assertive and communicate your concerns in an open and respectful way. If you've got an exam to study for and your chatty roommate just got home, say up front that you only have five minutes to talk. If you don't voice your feelings, resentment will build and the stress will increase.

Be willing to compromise. When you ask someone to change their behavior, be willing to do the same. If you both are willing to bend at least a little, you'll have a good chance of finding a happy middle ground.

Create a balanced schedule. All work and no play are a recipe for burnout. Try to find a balance between work and family life, social activities and solitary pursuits, daily responsibilities and downtime.

Adapt to the stressor

If you can't change the stressor, change yourself. You can adapt to stressful situations and regain your sense of control by changing your expectations and attitude.

Reframe problems. Try to view stressful situations from a more positive perspective. Rather than fuming about a traffic jam, look at it as an opportunity to pause and regroup, listen to your favorite radio station, or enjoy some time alone.

Look at the big picture. Take perspective of the stressful situation. Ask yourself how important it will be in the long run. Will it matter in a month? A year? Is it really worth getting upset over? If the answer is no, focus your time and energy elsewhere.

Adjust your standards. Perfectionism is a major source of avoidable stress. Stop setting yourself up for failure by demanding perfection. Set reasonable standards for yourself and others, and learn to be okay with "good enough."

Practice gratitude. When stress is getting you down, take a moment to reflect on all the things you appreciate in your life, including your own positive qualities and gifts. This simple strategy can help you keep things in perspective.

Accept the things you can't change

Some sources of stress are unavoidable. You can't prevent or change stressors such as the death of a loved one, a serious illness, or a national recession. In such cases, the best way to cope with stress is to accept things as they are. Acceptance may be difficult, but in the long run, it's easier than railing against a situation you can't change.

Don't try to control the uncontrollable. Many things in life are beyond our control, particularly the behavior of other people. Rather than stressing out over them, focus on the things you can control such as the way you choose to react to problems.

Look for the upside. When facing major challenges, try to look at them as opportunities for personal growth. If your own poor choices contributed to a stressful situation, reflect on them and learn from your mistakes.

Learn to forgive. Accept the fact that we live in an imperfect world and that people make mistakes. Let go of anger and resentments. Free yourself from negative energy by forgiving and moving on.

Share your feelings. Expressing what you're going through can be very cathartic, even if there's nothing you can do to alter the stressful situation. Talk to a trusted friend or make an appointment with a therapist.

Tip 3: Get moving

When you're stressed, the last thing you probably feel like doing is getting up and exercising. Interestingly physical activity is a huge stress reliever in fact you don't have to be an athlete or spend hours in a gym to experience the benefits. Exercise releases endorphins that make you feel good, and it can also serve as a valuable distraction from your daily worries.

While you'll get most of the benefits from regularly exercising for 30 minutes or more, it's okay to build up your fitness level gradually. Even very small activities can add up over the course of the day. The first step is to get yourself

123

up and moving. Here are some easy ways to incorporate exercise into your daily schedule:

- Put on some music and dance around.
- Walk or cycle to the grocery store.
- Use the stairs at home or work rather than an elevator.
- Park your car in the farthest spot in the lot and walk the rest of the way.
- Pair up with an exercise partner and encourage each other as you work out.
- Play ping-pong or an activity-based video game with others.

The stress-busting magic of mindful rhythmic exercise

While just about any form of physical activity can help burn away tension and stress, rhythmic activities are especially effective. Good choices include walking, running, swimming, dancing, cycling, tai chi, and aerobics. But whatever you choose, make sure it's something you enjoy so you're more likely to stick with it.

While you're exercising, make a conscious effort to pay attention to your body and the physical (and sometimes emotional) sensations you experience as you're moving. Focus on coordinating your breathing with your movements, or notice how the air or sunlight feels on your skin. Adding this mindfulness element will help you break out of the cycle of negative thoughts that often accompanies overwhelming stress.

Tip 4: Connecting with others

There is nothing more calming than spending quality time with another human being who makes you feel safe and understood. In fact, face-to-face interaction triggers a cascade of hormones that counteracts the body's defensive "fight-or-flight" response. Its nature's natural stress reliever (as an added bonus, it also helps stave off depression and anxiety). So, make it a point to connect regularly, and in person, with family and friends.

Keep in mind that the people you talk to don't have to be able to fix your stress. They simply need to be good listeners. And try not to let worries about looking weak or being a burden keep you from opening up. The people who care about you will be flattered by your trust. It will only strengthen your bond.

Of course, it's not always realistic to have a pal close by to lean on when you feel overwhelmed by stress, but by building and maintaining a network of close friends you can improve your resiliency to life's stressors.

Tip 5: Make time for fun and relaxation

Beyond a take-charge approach and a positive attitude, you can reduce stress in your life by carving out "me" time. Don't get so caught up in the hustle and bustle of life that you forget to take care of your own needs. Nurturing yourself is a necessity, not a luxury. If you regularly make time for fun and relaxation, you'll be in a better place to handle life's stressors.

Set aside leisure time. Include rest and relaxation in your daily schedule. Don't allow other obligations to encroach. This is your time to take a break from all responsibilities and recharge your batteries.

Do something you enjoy every day. Make time for leisure activities that bring you joy, whether it be stargazing, playing the piano, or working on your bike.

Keep your sense of humor. This includes the ability to laugh at yourself. The act of laughing helps your body fight stress in a number of ways.

Take up a relaxation practice. Relaxation techniques such as yoga, meditation, and deep breathing activate the body's relaxation response, a state of restfulness that is the opposite of the fight or flight or mobilization stress response. As you learn and practice these techniques, your stress levels will decrease and your mind and body will become calm and centered.

Tip 6: Manage your time better

Poor time management can cause a lot of stress. When you're stretched too thin and running behind, it's hard to stay calm and focused. Plus, you'll be tempted to avoid or cut back on all the healthy things you should be doing to keep stress in check, like socializing and getting enough sleep. The good news: there are things you can do to achieve a healthier work-life balance.

Don't over-commit yourself. Avoid scheduling things back-to-back or trying to fit too much into one day. All too often, we underestimate how long things will take.

Prioritize tasks. Make a list of tasks you have to do, and tackle them in order of importance. Do the high-priority items first. If you have something particularly unpleasant or stressful to do, get it over with early. The rest of your day will be more pleasant as a result.

Break projects into small steps. If a large project seems overwhelming, make a step-by-step plan. Focus on one manageable step at a time, rather than taking on everything at once.

Delegate responsibility. You don't have to do it all yourself, whether at home, school, or on the job. If other people can take care of the task, why not let them? Let go of the desire to control or oversee every little step. You'll be letting go of unnecessary stress in the process.

Tip 7: Maintain balance with a healthy lifestyle

In addition to regular exercise, there are other healthy lifestyle choices that can increase your resistance to stress.

Eat a healthy diet. Well-nourished bodies are better prepared to cope with stress; so be mindful of what you eat. Start your day right with breakfast, and keep your energy up and your mind clear with balanced, nutritious meals throughout the day.

Reduce caffeine and sugar. The temporary "highs" caffeine and sugar provide often end with a crash in mood and energy. By reducing the amount of coffee, soft drinks, chocolate, and sugar snacks in your diet, you'll feel more relaxed and you'll sleep better.

Avoid alcohol, cigarettes, and drugs. Self-medicating with alcohol or drugs may provide an easy escape from stress, but the relief is only temporary. Don't avoid or mask the issue at hand; deal with problems head on and with a clear mind.

Get enough sleep. Adequate sleep fuels your mind, as well as your body. Feeling tired will increase your stress because it may cause you to think irrationally.

Tip 8: Learn to relieve stress in the moment

When you're frazzled by your morning commute, or get stuck in a stressful meeting at work, or get upset from an argument with your spouse, you need a way to manage your stress levels right now. That's where quick stress relief comes in.

The fastest way to reduce stress is by taking a deep breath and using your senses—what you see, hear, taste, and touch, or through a soothing movement. By viewing a favorite photo, smelling a specific scent, listening to a favorite piece of music, tasting a piece of gum, or hugging a pet, for example, you can quickly relax and focus yourself.

Of course, not everyone responds to each sensory experience in the same way. The key to quick stress relief is to experiment and discover the unique sensory experiences that work best for you.

Creating routines

There are few things that impact your productivity, creativity, happiness, and career trajectory like building solid routines and habits. Now that we've developed a clear picture of our dreams, it's time that we make certain habits and set routines so that we can become more consistent day by day and reach our destination without much of a hassle.

We all know that creating a daily routine is essential, but getting to implement it is the hard part. If you look into most successful peoples' lives, you will realize that they follow a fixed schedule, which has helped them to build productivity habits over time. Creating a system that works and following it every day is an excellent way of becoming your best self. A successful routine gives you a laser-like focus from the moment you get up to the time you go to sleep.

According to studies, up to 40% of our daily actions are powered by habits. Meaning your subconscious mind can either work for you or against you? But you don't need studies to tell you how powerful the right habits can be. Whole books have been filled with the daily routines of successful entrepreneurs, innovators, and creatives.

We are what we repeatedly do. Excellence, then, is not an act, but a habit.

– Aristotle

So, if you're ready to become the best version of you and put your productivity on "autopilot", let us debunk some of the common misconceptions around creating habits and routines and then guide you through a simple process for designing your perfect day.

You might be familiar with the saying *"good is the enemy of great."* And in a lot of cases, it might seem like following a daily routine and schedule is simply defaulting to *"good enough."* When you follow a routine, you're losing the excitement and spontaneity you need to be truly creative, right?

Not really. In fact, our world is already too full of spontaneity and excitement for our own good.

The only way you can do justice to your work is by putting in time. Writers have to write, coders need to code, designers need to design. Unfortunately, that's getting harder to do. Social media, entertainment, and the news (not to mention "productive" distractions like spending all day on chat or email!) suck away at our attention like vampires. On the other hand, success comes from hard work, commitment, and a dedication put in work even when you don't want to. As Stanford behavioral scientist B. J. Fogg states:

"If you pick the right small behavior and sequence, it's right, then you won't have to motivate yourself to have it grow. It will just happen naturally, like a good seed planted in a good spot."

More specifically, a routine helps you in a number of ways:

● **Routines help you prioritize what's important.** When you schedule your day a certain way or work hard to build specific habits, you're essentially saying "this is what's important to me." Routines and habits force you to think hard about your priorities and make choices.

● **Knowing what you're doing each day helps you block distractions.** As the best-selling author, Nir Eyal writes, *"You can't say you're distracted if you don't know what you're distracted from."* When you have a routine, you're more likely to notice when something is trying to take away your attention.

● **Habits free up energy for more important tasks.** The reason 40% of our actions are driven by habit is that our minds love to conserve energy. The more you can automate the things you do each day, the more mental space and energy you have to commit to more important tasks.

● **Daily routines and habits boost creativity.** As we wrote in our Guide to Being More Creative, there's no such thing as a creative muse. Instead, the most creative ideas come from working consistently and putting in the time.

● **Habits and routines drive you forward**. More than anything, your habits and routines are what help you see progress and motivate you to do more.

Difference between Habit and Routine:

A habit is an action or behavior you've turned into an automatic response. Something triggers you (either externally like a notification, or internally like a certain feeling) and you're compelled to follow it through.

A routine, on the other hand, is a string of habits you create for specific parts of the day. Maybe it's a morning routine you do when you first wake up. Or an afternoon routine to help you get over the post-lunch dip. Whatever it is, we all have these routines. But we don't all realize how powerful they are.

Everyone has got their own thing

If our lives and our success depends on our routines and habits, then why not just follow the paths laid out by other people?
Successful founders and creators love to talk about how they spend their day and share the "secrets" of their productivity. But there's a problem with simply trying to retrace their steps: Just because a routine works for someone else,

doesn't mean it will work for you. More than just following other people's daily routines and habits, the best way to become the best version of yourself is to question, experiment, and learn what works for you.

The big caveat here is that the routine has to match the person performing it. We all have different triggers for habits, levels of willpower, and autonomy over how we spend our time. And assuming you're exactly the same as someone like Elon Musk and following his routine blindly, is a perfect recipe for disaster.

Instead, you need to experiment for yourself to optimize your own day. More specifically, there are a few areas of your life you should look to build solid habits and develop productive daily routines:

- Your Morning Routine
- Work Habits to help you stay focused
- Disconnecting from work
- Optimizing for energy and health

Ways to become highly productive

You've undoubtedly heard that the most productive people wake up early. Whether its author Haruki Murakami, getting up at 4:00 AM to write or Apple CEO Tim Cook, starting his day at 3:45 AM to get through his email. But that's not all it takes to build a productive morning routine.

Here are a few habits that you can develop to make the most out of yourselves:

MORNING ROUTINES (Starting your day)

1. Giving yourself more time by waking up earlier

English academic Richard Whately once observed, *"Lose an hour in the morning, and you will spend all day looking for it."*

There's a reason you keep seeing early wake-up times for highly successful people. Most of them realize that by the time 9 AM rolls around and the rest of the world has woken up, their time isn't just theirs anymore. Early mornings are a chance to prepare for the day, spend time on meaningful projects, or even get in some more family time. All things that will help you stay focused and motivated for the rest of the day.

But more than just setting an early alarm, building a habit of getting up early requires a few considerations.

First, you can't sacrifice your sleep. Getting up earlier means going to bed earlier. And a lack of sleep (less than 6-8 hours) will do far more harm than the good of getting up early.

Next, you need to be consistent with your wake-up time. Our bodies crave consistency and so do our habits. The more you're able to stick to specific wake-up times, the more likely you'll be able to turn this into a solid habit.

Lastly, never, ever hit snooze. As Benjamin Spall, co-author of My Morning Routine: How Successful People Start Every Day Inspired, writes:

"Highly productive people don't hit the snooze button. They just don't. This has been the most consistent theme that's come up in my over five years of interviewing people about their mornings. They do, however, set an alarm to hedge against oversleeping, even if they end up waking up and turning it off before it has a chance to sound."

2. Making your bed

Not all habits need to be major changes and sometimes it's the small acts that have the biggest returns. At least that's what Four Hour Workweek author and investor Tim Ferriss believes.

Tim swears by the simple act of making your bed in the morning. Not only does this start your day out on a positive note, but it can create a chain of accomplishment that motivates you to keep working throughout the day.

Plus, as Tim writes, even though building a habit of making your bed might seem easy, it gives you a sense of control you can take with you:

"No matter how bad your day is, no matter how catastrophic it might become, you can make your bed."

3. Setting your Most Important Tasks for the Day

A major goal of any productive morning routine is to set your intention and tone for the day. Do you want to feel focused or scattered? Are you attacking the day with a purpose or just reacting to other people?

Controlling the narrative for your day is the best way to be more productive throughout. And one of the easiest ways to do this is to start your day by defining your Most Important Tasks (MITs).

Here's how Zen Habits founder Leo Babauta explains the idea of MITs:

"Your MIT is the task you most want or need to get done today. In my case, I've tweaked it a bit so that I have three MITs, the three things I must accomplish today. Do I get a lot more done than three things? Of course. But the idea is that no matter what else I do today, these are the things I want to be sure of doing."

Writing these at the start of your day means you're thinking about them with a clear head and not being influenced by distractions or interruptions. Your MITs give you a map of what a successful day will look like.

4. Connecting with your bigger goals by journaling

Journaling isn't just for angsty highschoolers. In fact, the act of writing and reflecting on your goals, dreams, and even feelings has been found to improve your mood and even help you perform better at work.

According to Harvard Business School psychologist Francesca Gino, this is because reflecting on your work reminds you that, you are good at it.

When people have the opportunity to reflect, they experience a boost in self-efficacy. They feel more confident that they can achieve things. As a result, they put more effort into what they're doing.

How you choose to reflect can come in many different forms. For some people, it's all about re-writing your goals to home in on what's most important. While

132

others opt for writing and reciting positive affirmations to boost self-confidence. If those feel a bit too "self-help-y" for you, there are a few other options:

First, there's the Five-Minute Journal, a simple notebook that asks you to set your intentions and reflect on things you're grateful for. Or, you can use something like 750 words or the Morning Pages process; a system for writing 3 pages first thing in the morning to get rid of lingering thoughts and set you out with a clear head.

5. Meditating to prepare for whatever the day brings

You don't always know what the day is going to throw at you. But adding a habit of meditation to your morning routine helps train you to deal with things in a better and calmer way. I've plethora of content related to mediation on my YouTube channel and I suggest you to check it out by using this URL:

https://www.youtube.com/prriyasuccessacademy

If you're new to meditation, it's important to start small. Like any new habit, consistency is more important than intensity at the start. Even simply sitting in a quiet room with your eyes closed for a few minutes and focusing on your breath can be enough to get you started.

WORK-DAY ROUTINES (The essential workday habits that keep you focused and productive)

While your morning routine sets you up for a productive day, you can also optimize your daily routines and how you spend your time during the workday.

Rather than just reacting to what's being thrown at you, productive workday habits and routines make sure you know and focus on your priorities, can block out distractions, and have a plan for getting back on track when things go awry.

Here are a few habits to experiment with when developing your workday routine:

6. Skipping email first thing in the morning:

Our brain hates the unknown. And so, whether you glance at your phone and see a bunch of red dots besides your email and chat apps or have your inbox open in the background (like 84% of people!) you probably feel compelled to check your messages first.

However, what all this does is, make you spend your day reacting to other people's needs instead of working on your own. As Farnham Street founder, Shane Parrish, says:

'If I got up in the morning and the first thing I did was check my email, I'd be allowing others to dictate my priorities for the day.'

Try to build a habit of setting aside the first hour or more of your day without email or chat. Don't accept morning meetings and leave your inbox closed and instead work on one of your MITs that you wrote before work. This way, you can make progress on meaningful work and build a habit of committing to your priorities.

7. Eating the frog (tackle something difficult when your energy is at its peak)

We all go through regular ebbs and flows of energy, focus, and productivity throughout the day. And while this cycle is different for everyone, most of us have a spike first thing in the morning (and not just due to coffee!) This is a perfect time to build the habit of eating the frog. Wait, what? No, you're not going to eat an actual live animal. Instead, this simply means crossing off one of those nagging tasks that has been hanging over you.

As Mark Twain famously wrote:

"Eat a live frog first thing in the morning and nothing worse will happen to you the rest of the day."

Maybe this means getting back to an awkward email from a stakeholder, tackling an especially annoying bug, or writing a scope of work for an outside contractor. The goal is simply to get it done so you're not distracted by it during the rest of your day.

8. Scheduling (and take) more breaks

Sticking with this idea of working with your body's natural energy curves, we can't be productive all the time.

In fact, studies into our changing energy levels uncovered something researchers call Ultradian Rhythms. These are 90–120-minute sessions of alertness that our mind cycles through before needing a break.

According to sleep researcher Nathaniel Kleitman, our minds naturally crave breaks after every 90 minutes of intense work. Even worse, when you work when your body wants to rest, it uses our reserve stores of energy to keep up. This means releasing stress hormones to give us an extra kick of energy.

A better answer is to actually take breaks when you need them. Listen to your body and schedule regular breaks away from your screen at least every 90 minutes.

If you want to make the most out of these breaks make sure you get out of your chair, take a brisk walk, and try to spend a bit of time around nature as these have all been found to quickly help us rejuvenate and recharge our energy.

9. "Batching" similar work together

Like most people, you probably wear a lot of hats at work. Your title might be a project manager or designer or developer, but your day is full of all sorts of different work. In fact, as one study from researchers at Wharton found:

"At many companies the proportion hovers around 80%, leaving employees little time for all the critical work they must complete on their own."

This kind of constant context switching kills your ability to focus and to be productive. Every time your brain switches to a different task it can take up to 15 minutes for it to get back into the previous task. Jump around 4 times and you've lost an entire hour of work.

That's where building a habit of "batching" becomes so important. As entrepreneur and author Paul Jarvis explains:

'Batching' builds off the idea of only working on one kind of task at a time. Rather than jumping from one project to another, you do all related tasks in a set amount of time.

Look at your schedule. Are there spaces where you can set aside some heads-down time to batch important work? Try to find at least one 90-minute chunk where you can push distractions aside and power through your MITs.

10. Setting hard limits on certain activities

No matter how well you've built habits and routines around focused work, you'll undoubtedly fall off the ladder from time to time. The issue is that many of us have bad habits we've built over the years that creep in when we're most vulnerable.

Maybe it's getting sucked into social media first thing in the morning. Or watching too many YouTube videos after lunch. Or maybe even staying up late to watch movies and missing out on sleep. Whatever it is, you need to break those habits if you want to be truly productive. For artist and writer Alex Mathers, the solution was to create a list of rules and hard limits around his time on 'distracting' activities. Rather than a set routine, his rules act as guardrails for his motivation each day.

By reading through your own rules first thing in the morning, you become aware of what your priorities are and can catch yourself when you go off them. As an added bonus, use a time-tracking tool to see exactly how much time you're spending on certain activities and get alerts when you go over.

11. Scheduling your email and IM time (or create "office hours")

Email can take over your life if you let it. And one of the worst workplace habits you need to break is, constantly checking it. Even if you built a habit of skipping email first thing in the morning, you need to control when you let it into the rest of your day.

In fact, according to one study of over 50,000 knowledge workers, most can't go 6 minutes without checking their email or IM tool!

There's no perfect answer to the question of how often you should check your email. But most productivity experts agree that the best habit to build is to be active with your email and not just react to it.

Time management expert Elizabeth Grace Saunders only checks her email once a day (to make her daily schedule). While New York Times best-selling author, Mark Murphy, says you should take at least a 2-hour break from email once a day. Think of this as your personal "office hours." These are the times where you're available to communicate and collaborate. But the rest of the time is pure, email-free bliss. No desktop notifications. No checks on your phone. Just time for focused work.

12. Using GTD to build a habit of staying organized

As we said at the top of this post, you can't be focused if you don't know what you're distracted from. And having a system for staying organized is one of the most foundational workplace habits and routines you can build.

While it takes a bit of effort to start up and stick with it, you can't go wrong with the Getting Things Done (GTD) productivity system from David Allen.

As we wrote in us How to Use GTD in 2019 guide, GTD is made up of 3 stages:

1. The intake stage is where you collect and clarify tasks, projects, and ideas.
2. Next, there's an 'organization and prioritization' stage where you decide what to work on, when, and set deadlines and reminders to keep you on track.
3. Finally, you move onto an action stage where you work through your priorities and, as the name says, get things done.

When built into your daily routine, GTD can be a life-changing habit.

WHEN YOU HAVE SPARE TIME (Disconnecting from work)

Long days are inevitable. But if you want to be truly productive, your habits and routines can't end when the workday does. Instead, research has consistently found that people who follow an end-of-day routine are less fatigued and stressed, show lower rates of procrastination, and even become more focused during the workday.

Here are a few habits you can try to build your own productive end-of-day routines:

13. Reflecting on your accomplishments and writing down three good things that happened

It's all too easy to finish your day and try to 'relax' with Netflix. Unfortunately, the human brain doesn't just switch gears like that. Instead, when left undealt with, thoughts and emotions linger and pop up at the worst times (like when you're trying to go to sleep!)

One way to help de-stress from the workday is with a personal debrief. Especially one that focuses on your accomplishments and the positive things that happened to you. Build this routine for long enough and it can even change the way you perceive your days and help you not get sucked into the negative.

As Shawn Achor, author of The Happiness Advantage, explains:

"When you write down a list of 'three good things' that happened that day, your brain will be forced to scan the last 24 hours for potential positive—things that brought small or large laughs, feelings of accomplishment at work, a strengthened connection with family, a glimmer of hope for the future. In just five minutes a day, this trains the brain to become more skilled at noticing and focusing on possibilities for personal and professional growth and seizing opportunities to act on them."

14. Making space for mental solitude

We're naturally social creatures. However, all that time with people takes its toll. A bit of solitude as everyone from Thoreau to Proust have written about is one of our most powerful tools for disconnecting and recharging. This doesn't mean you need to lock yourself away in a room at the end of the day. But rather just find a bit of 'mental solitude' in your evening routine.

As Deep Work author, Cal Newport writes:

"The key to solitude is to step away from reacting to the output of other minds: be it listening to a podcast, scanning social media, reading a book, watching TV or holding an actual conversation.

Spending time isolated from other minds is what allows you to process and regulate complex emotions. It's the only time you can refine the principles on which you can build a life of character. It's what allows you to crack hard problems, and is often necessary for creative insight. If you avoid time alone with your brain your mental life will be much more fragile and much less productive."

Take a few minutes after work to separate yourself from other thoughts and ideas and dig into your own. If you want, write down ideas, thoughts, and feelings that won't leave you alone. This way, you know everything is ready to be dealt with tomorrow, and you can be free to truly relax and recover.

15. Spending time on a hobby

One of the more counter-intuitive habits that can actually help you recover and be more productive is to do more work at home. Rather than just relaxing, engaging in what's called a mastery task helps you disconnect from the workday and be more energized and focused for the following day.

As Alex Soojung-Kim Pang, author of Rest: Why You Get More Done When You Work Less, explains:

Mastery experiences are engaging, interesting things that you do well. They're often challenging, but this makes them mentally absorbing and all the more rewarding when they're proficiently executed.

To get even more from your mastery activities, look for hobbies that include other people (to fulfill our social needs), are healthy (like sports or exercise), or give you space to think and be alone (to bring even more mental solitude).

16. Preparing for tomorrow with a 'shutdown ritual'

Not everyone has total control over how they spend their time during the workday, which can often mean we get stuck being upset with how things didn't go as planned. However, creating a sense of control is an important part of calming your brain and staying positive and productive.

In his book, Drive: The Surprising Truth about what Motivates Us, Daniel Pink suggests creating a 'shutdown ritual' that gives you back that sense of control, no matter what happened during the day:

Establish a closing ritual. Know when to stop working. Try to end each work day the same way, too. Straighten up your desk. Backup your computer. Make a list of what you need to do tomorrow.

You get to choose your own ritual. But a few elements that have been shown to help include:

- Writing your to-do list for tomorrow

- Reflecting on your day and writing in a journal

- Closing open browser tabs and cleaning your desktop

- Setting out clothes for the morning (or the gym)

17. Turning off your devices at least 30 minutes before bed

A lack of sleep ruins everything. It doesn't matter how productive you're being in other aspects of your life, if you don't get a solid night's sleep all those efforts are wasted. Unfortunately, getting proper sleep isn't just about the time you give yourself.

The blue light that is emitted from the screens of our devices can mess with your internal clock and make it more difficult to fall asleep. According to Dr. Adrian Williams, professor of sleep medicine:

"The influence of light on hormonal responses is minimal in the day, but maximal in the evening when it may suppress melatonin secretion and delay sleep."

While stopping your screen time a few hours before bed is preferable, most experts agree that you stop at least 30-minutes before you go to bed.

If you want to make building this habit even easier (and give yourself some added benefits), simply leave your phone outside of the bedroom. This way, you won't be tempted to check it and you'll have a better morning by not waking up to a screen full of notifications.

GENERAL ROUTINES (optimizing energy and health)

Not all great productive habits fit into specific parts of our day, and not every routine has to do with how you spend your time at work. How our bodies feel affects our ability to focus and be productive, and ignoring your health isn't an option when you want to build a productive routine.

As much as possible, you should try and work these few habits into your daily routine.

18. Giving your eyes a break

You probably spend a terrifying amount of your day staring at a screen. So much so that there's actually a condition called computer vision syndrome that occurs in 50-90% of knowledge workers. When your eyes become fatigued it can have a far-reaching impact, from physical fatigue, decreased productivity, and increased errors, to minor irritations like eye twitching.

There are lots of ways you can protect your eyes during the day like using proper lighting, reducing screen glare, and taking more breaks. However, one of the easiest habits to build is to follow the "20-20-20 rule".

Every 20 minutes of time spent staring at a screen, look away at an option that is at least 20 feet away for 20 seconds.

Another exercise is to look far away at an object for 10-15 seconds, then gaze at something up close for 10-15 seconds. Then look back at the distant object. Do this 10 times to stop your eyes from "locking up" during the day.

19. Drinking more water during the day

Water is a miracle productivity tool. Yet most of us skip the water cooler and head for the coffee machine when we're feeling a lack of energy.

And while caffeine definitely has its place in our workday. Drinking more water is one of the best daily routines you can build. Our bodies run on water, and dehydration doesn't just result in a dry mouth but causes a lack of energy, focus, motivation, and productivity.

To stay properly hydrated during the day, build a habit of drinking water. Carry a water bottle with you as a reminder to drink more or set a goal for the day.

20. Regular exercise

Lastly, you don't need another person telling you the benefits of exercise. But I'm going to do it anyway. If your physical health and having a beach body isn't as much of a priority to you, then listen to these other results.

Exercise can slow down neurogenesis, meaning you'll keep more brain cells as you age. Over a shorter timeframe, it can also give you more energy throughout the day, keep you happy and motivated to work more, and even help you stay mentally focused for longer.

Building exercise into your daily routine doesn't have to be a huge endeavor. In their book, '*Make Time: How to Focus on What Matters Every Day*', authors John Zeratksy and Jake Knapp explain how modern culture encourages unrealistic expectations about exercise:

"Moving your body is the best way to charge your battery. But you don't need lengthy complicated workouts."

Instead, the authors suggest a few simple rules:

- **Exercise for about 20 minutes:** Research shows the most important cognitive results can come from just 20 minutes of exercise.
- **Do it every day:** The energy and mood boost from exercise lasts about a day, so it's important to keep up with your routine.
- **Don't stress about perfection:** If you do 4 out of 7 days, that's great. The goal is consistency over the long-term. Not stressing that you missed a day here or there.

This means your routine could be going to the gym for a quick workout, doing some body weight exercises in the office, or even just going for a brisk walk and taking the stairs each day. Like best daily routines, it's about being able to do it consistently.

Daily routines are just guidelines for living your best life

All of the previously mentioned habits and tips will help you be more productive. Although, trying to add all of them to your daily routine is probably a bad idea. Instead, you need to experiment and see what works for you. Try one every week and track your results. Does it work? Why not?

Ultimately, we'll always default to doing what works best for us. Your body and mind will tell you if certain things aren't working for you (you'll get restless, bored, anxious, tired, etc…). Listen to those signs and use them to build your own personalized daily routine.

Until then,

Prriya Kaur

"20 years from now you will be more disappointed by the things that you didn't do than by the ones you did do. So, throw off the bowlines. Sail away from the safe harbor. Catch the trade winds in your sails. Explore. Dream. Discover."

– Mark Twain

Some heads up for the next day: *Tomorrow we'll be covering up a really important aspect of life, how to use money as a financial tool and the relation between knowledge and wealth.*

Day Five/Step Five

Building the foundations of wealth

Understanding the dynamics of money and its usage as a financial tool

BEFORE STARTING OFF WITH TODAY

• **Take a while to go through the Self-image Reformulation exercise from day one.**

• **Go through this daily affirmation:**

I am born to succeed, the infinite within me cannot fail. The divine law and order govern my life, divine peace fill my soul, and divine love saturates my mind.

Infinite intelligence guides me in all ways, God's riches flow to me freely. I am advancing, moving forward and growing mentally, spiritually, financially and in other ways.

I know these truths are sinking into my subconscious mind and will grow after their kind, today is God's Day. I chose happiness, success, prosperity and peace of mind.

All I need is within me.

1. Recall your purpose of life, ambitions and goals from day four.

2. To reinvigorate yourself, choose from any routine methods -preferably the meditation one from 'The ways to be highly productive' section mentioned in day four.

3. Select any exercise from day two and three which you like and condition your mind to get started for today.

There was once a nuclear plant that went offline all of sudden and it completely wrecked the power infrastructure of a nearby city. The government body that maintained the plant, started to lose millions per day in revenue, and also put the other lucrative government subsidies at risk.

They tried really hard to find the right person who can be consulted to resolve the matter and if possible, eventually fix the issue as well. As time went by, they finally came across a really experienced expert who was by chance in the town for a conference. So, the authorities contacted the expert, and pleaded him to come by and take a look.

Once onsite, the expert looked around for a few minutes and after a while, he pulled out a hammer from his bag. He gently taped on one of the valves and the pipe it was attached to, and within a fraction of seconds he instructed the officials to check the status of the reactor.

To the amazement of all the officials present in the vicinity, the reactor came to life!

The next day, an invoice from the expert for $500,000 was presented to the Supervising Directors of the nuclear plant. Confounded, the directors call the expert and yell, "Do you seriously expect us to pay you half a million dollars for tapping the wall with a hammer?!?!" To which the expert replied, "No. It's $1 for tapping the wall, and $499,999 for knowing where to tap it."

The wealth around you

In my seminars, I often say that making money is relatively easy and yet most folks never achieve financial independence in the first place. In fact, most people retire poor. I consider that a modern tragedy, and one of my goals is to change that! You can retire with "enough" – you can earn more, and more importantly, you can keep more! Let's talk about how.

Accumulating wealth is the predictable result of knowledge, effective strategies, patience and persistence. If other people have done it, you can, too! Let's figure out how.

The essential first step is to respect money and understand how it works. Most people never study money. Some of us even avoid the subject. We don't talk about it in our families. We don't read about it; we don't budget or track it, and we certainly don't teach our children about it in school, which I think is a terrible mistake. No wonder that as adults, the one thing we do know about money is that we don't have enough of it! It's time to change that!

The second step to creating wealth is to understand this: Money is fundamentally an idea!

It's a social agreement to exchange value in a convenient way. Little pieces of paper with pictures and numbers have no inherent value. After World War I, particularly in Germany, cash literally became worthless. There are famous stories of a woman with a wheelbarrow full of cash going to buy bread. Some thieves accosted her, wrestled the wheelbarrow from her, turned it over to dump the money on the ground and ran off with the wheelbarrow.

People had lost faith in their money, and it no longer had any value.

The key to making money is understanding that those numbers and pieces of paper represent human effort and wealth. We can exchange pieces of paper for goods and services only if we agree that those pieces of paper represent value!

Money is a social contract, an agreement about value. And so, the price of any object is only what two people – a willing buyer and a willing seller – decide its worth. I might decide that a particular piece of paper is worth almost nothing to me, because it has value only as a bookmark or note paper. But to the seller, it may be a valuable stock certificate, or a priceless painting. The value? It's entirely and literally, in the eye of the beholder.

To make and keep money, it is absolutely essential that you "get" this! Your home, your job, your car, the price of a meal in a restaurant or an airline ticket is only what the buyer and seller decide it is!

Take a moment to ponder that. In Germany, that woman's wheelbarrow was of far more "value" than the millions of dollars of printed money it contained. The money was worthless.

The value of money over the years

Hopefully, none of us will ever see our money become worthless, although in a sense that is what happens through inflation. Not too many years ago, as a society, we thought a loaf of bread was worth about 50 cents. Today, we generally agree to pay somewhere between two and four dollars, depending on things like freshness, packaging and special ingredients.

And that simple example holds the key to your getting rich! In my family, we pay more for a loaf of bread that contains whole wheat, is freshly baked, and that we have the "privilege" of slicing ourselves. Why would anyone pay more for unsliced bread? Because of our concept of "value". Keep that in mind!

It's only been in about the past hundred years that society has moved away from considering only gold and silver as "real" money. Credit cards, as we know them, were invented in the early 50's, shortly after WWII, and many subscribers to my weekly newsletter remember when credit cards were rare.

Today everyone accepts credit cards and electronic transfers as real, and the numbers printed on monthly statements from our banks and stock brokers can make us happy or very sad!

What does all this history and philosophy have to do with making you rich? I admit this may seem like a long detour, but I assure you, it is the key to getting rich!

Remember, in the last chapter, I wrote that money is an agreement about value. If you want more money, you must create something that other people value!

Throughout history, the things we value have changed. At one time, we valued animals, like cows or pigs. For centuries, horses were particularly valued for their mobility and value as a source of military power. Even before that, with the rise of agriculture, land was valued because we could use it to grow food, and the crops were extremely valuable. For many people today, land remains a primary source of value and they will pay a premium for a piece of ground on which to have a yard, perhaps a small garden and a sense of privacy. For others, however, land is of little value, and they live in apartments or condominiums.

By the 19th century, industrial capacity emerged as the primary source of value, and the richest people in the world owned railroads, oil refineries, and steel mills. The ability to produce "things" was the most valuable ability on earth, followed closely by the ability to sell or "retail" those things. Families like the Rockefellers made fortunes in oil, while Henry Ford created the modern assembly line and Macy's, J.C. Penney's and Sears & Roebucks created value (and wealth) by making products available to the average consumer.

In the past 25 year, however, attention has shifted again, and we now value information, and even more, the ability to use information to solve problems. That is the key to wealth!

The cost of starting something

When land was the primary measure of value, it was almost impossible for the average person to acquire wealth. The king owned all the land, and the population struggled to survive on what they could grow or earn in small cottage industries.

When manufacturing was the source of wealth, more people had access to great fortunes, but the number of millionaires was still small because it cost so much to build a factory or run railroad tracks across miles of wilderness. Few people could raise the capital, and so few people ever got into the game. For centuries, most people lived on wages and saved what they could, with very few ever achieving more than a modest level of savings and financial security. The barriers prevented most people from ever being able to own a business or take control of their financial future.

Think, Execute, Analyze (and make changes if needed), Repeat

–Shivendu Mishra

But today, the barriers to entry are essentially zero!

The pages you are now reading represent one of the greatest revolutions in human history.

Think about this for a moment....

Even 10 years ago, I might have written these pages, but the odds that you would be reading them were very slim. After writing the pages, I would have contacted a magazine or book editor with a hope that they would publish my writing, or I would have gone to a local printer, paid to have a few hundred copies of this book made up, and then announced that it was for sale.

But who would have bought it?

By the time I put an ad in a couple of magazines, or in the newspaper or on the radio, the cost of this book would have been several dollars, and you probably would have never heard about it, or decided it wasn't worth the price.

But today, I can put this together, publish it on my website or on various online bookstores, announce it to the world, and you would've had fairly easy access! The total cost of production? Some of my time, and the use of any word processing software to format it.

Importance of Value over money

There is an old saying, "The more you put in, the more you can take out". It means that you must first put the value. You must contribute something of worth, something that makes a difference, something your customers (your boss, your clients, and your community) value!

Value always comes first; money comes second.

And here's a paradoxical truth about getting rich: To make lots of money, you must sell your goods and services for less than what your customer believes its worth is! (Who would pay more than something is worth?)

Most of us get it backwards. We say, "Pay me more money, and I'll work harder or I'll go to school and add more value". But in economics, it never works that way.

Creating value is about changing (transforming) the quality or nature of something. It's about using earth, water, sun and seeds to grow valuable corn. It's about transforming an eager student into a skilled doctor. It's about turning a good idea into a useful tool. It's about putting this booklet on the Internet, making it available, making it useful, and creating value.

So, let's focus on adding tons of value! Everyone has the opportunity to add significant value. By using your skills to create a product or provide a service that makes life easier, more comfortable or more profitable, you create value. Or, by investing in someone else's company, you increase their ability to serve customers.

So, how will you do that? That is the only question.

Less than a generation ago, there were other questions. Examples included: Will the union get me a raise? Will they add dental care to my health insurance benefits this year? Teachers asked when they would receive tenure, and engineers asked about the company's retirement benefits. Those were valid questions only a few years ago. Today, they no longer apply.

No matter what your skill, someone is working very hard to provide the benefits of what you do at a cheaper price. Let's pick an extreme example. You might think that brain surgeons could count on significant income, but even that is no longer true. Pharmaceutical companies are racing to produce drugs

153

that reduce the need for surgery, or that prevent illness altogether. Managed care companies now routinely prohibit operations that only a few years ago were common. In fact, the need for specialists of all types, including neuro-surgeons, is actually going down!

There is no such thing as job security! Someone, somewhere is working very hard to eliminate your current job, or to reduce your income.

The key, the only key is: provide value!

To become wealthy, all you have to do is provide a benefit that lots of people value. How do you do that? Generally, by giving people something they want, or by removing something they don't want.

One of the most successful businesses no one ever heard of during the 90's was "SafetyKleen". They haul away the waste oil and solvents from gas stations and repair shops. It's dirty, disgusting stuff and no one wants to touch it! So, people value the service of having someone take it away. It's a great example of providing value by eliminating a problem.

Check out their stock chart over the past few years. Lots of folks got very, very rich!

Johnson & Johnson has become a multi-national company largely on the basis of eliminating headaches (they sell Tylenol brand that relieves pain). Proctor & Gamble removes dirt from our clothes (Tide detergent) and plaque from our teeth (Crest toothpaste). The point? People will pay you to solve their problems!

Attorneys solve problems. Real Estate agents solve problems. Dentists, doctors, chiropractors and fitness centers eliminate or prevent problems and people value these services!

Or, provide a pleasure people value! Walt Disney made people laugh, and he laughed all the way to the bank! Fax machines and email save us time and postage, so we value them and both fax machines and email software (and often, extra telephone lines!) are standard equipment in every office and in many of our homes. McDonalds and other fast-food restaurants do not serve great food, but they do serve convenience, reliable, predictable service, and speed. In our hurry-up culture, these are things that we value, and they have made the McDonalds restaurant chain (and their stockholders) very, very rich.

The possibilities are unlimited, but you must provide value, and you must take action!

Law of attraction and Money

Given the opportunity, everyone would love to accumulate more wealth, make more money, and live an abundant life. However, many people have a poor relationship with money. They have trouble **manifesting money** and wealth into their lives, and as a result, never achieve the financial success they desire.

The truth is that financial success starts in the mind and the number one thing holding many people back is their belief system concerning wealth and money.

With that in mind, leveraging the **Law of Attraction** is one of the most effective ways to change your beliefs about money into a belief system that will open you up to the prosperity that is all around you. Those who have already discovered the explosive potential within the Law of Attraction and changed their lives for the better, as well as those who are looking to uncover more about the law for the first time, usually have one thing in common.

"Their focal point is probably to use The Law of Attraction for having more money and being wealthy."

In today's society, being driven by a need for extraordinary wealth is often associated with greed and selfishness. The majority of us are programmed from childhood to believe that the richest amongst us are exceptional in some way, or have obtained great wealth through negative means or extreme sacrifice.

However, for those who have harnessed the Law of Attraction combined with a rich person mentality and applied it to achieve these levels of incredible wealth-income has not necessarily been their ultimate aim.

When we are looking to live out our dreams and obtain all that we want, be it good health, a business you are passionate about, a happy marriage, or a life of traveling; the fact is financial freedom must usually be obtained first. With total freedom, an individual is left free to focus all of their mental energies on what it is that they truly want from life.

They are free from the burdens and stress of bills, debts, and back-breaking work. Arguably, the biggest excuse used by large numbers of unsatisfied workers is that they are unable to live out their dreams as a result of a lack of cash flow.

"Imagination is everything; it is the preview of life coming attractions."

– Albert Einstein

Very few individuals enjoy the luxury of financial freedom. However, those who have, usually have one thing in common. They are positive thinkers. They have goals and they take action. This behavior is the backbone of The Law of Attraction.

Complete and utter faith in the Universe's ability to provide you with all that you envision in your mind and unfaltering gratitude for what you have already got is one step towards using the Law of Attraction properly.

Using the law to our advantage

I'm sure that the idea that you could attract cash among all the important things is what attracted you to the Law of Attraction. If so, you're not alone. Nearly every person wishes to discover just how to attract more cash utilizing Law of Attraction strategies.

Nevertheless, perhaps you've since found that methods to draw in the money are more complex than you expected. Alternatively, you probably believe that you have actually been doing all the appropriate things; however, you still have not quite identified just how to utilize the Law of Attraction to build the optimum wealth.

We'll be going through a bunch of ways that'll help you practice the law in a different way altogether, and likewise would tell us how to materialize money swiftly as well as easily making use of targeted meditations to bring in the abundance you've always wanted.

Lastly, we'll check out the best law of attraction wealth manifestation tricks. Prior to you recognizing it, you'll prepare to show up in the blink of an eye!

PRACTICING THE LAW OF ATTRACTION FOR WEALTH MANIFESTION IN A DIFFERENT WAY

1. Begin with gratefulness.

Always start with thanksgiving; be glad wherefore you currently have as well as see the wonders that originate from this simple act. Next, you have actually got to test on your own to create. Create much more concepts than you require for yourself so you can share and also give your concepts away.

That is called fruitfulness as well as abundance– it indicates dealing with producing greater than you require for yourself so you can begin blessing others, blessing your nation and also blessing your business.

When wealth starts ahead, when somebody becomes extremely effective, it's fantastic what the numbers end up being.

2. Law of Attraction Wealth – Fantasize it.

Whatever starts, starts in the heart and mind, every great achievement began in the mind of someone.

They risked desiring, and thought that it was possible. Take a while to enable yourself to ask, Suppose? Believe large. Do not let a negative attitude dissuade you.

You wish to be a "daydreamer." Dream of the possibilities for yourself, your family and also for others.

If you had a dream that you allowed to cool, re-ignite the desire! Follow the flames. Life is brief to let it go.

3. Alter your mindset.

Rich people stay in a globe of wealth. Poor individuals reside in a globe of restriction. Poor people think there's not nearly enough to go around on the planet. They originate from a fear-based attitude. Their answers are "either/or," but never "both."

In a poor person's state of mind, they opt for safety and security over love, security prior to self-expression, and security over opportunity. Abundant individuals recognize that with a little creativity, a determination to be unusual and also an open mind, they can have both. When you build your life on the "Both!" mentality, you will certainly see more possibilities. What about you? Are you an opportunity theorist or a fear-based thinker?

4. Create an equipping reality.

You're developing your truth right now, but chances are you're not being very intentional about the fact that you're developing.

Reality is subjective; if you understand that it's a construct, if you realize that you are picking to think something, after that you can pick to think that you can do something concerning it.

Write down the ideas that you have on your own.

On one side, checklist the things that encourage you and also move you forward, things that make you much more certain, that offer you the nerve and also the audacity to move on. Beyond, list the things that demotivate or demean you and also relocate you away from your goals.

You can pick to think things that encourage you, and you can pick to neglect things that relocate you backward. It's all a construct.

5. Stop making excuses.

Eliminating justifications is very important because your future is necessary.

If you only get the future that you benefit from, then what you provide is pretty crucial, ideal? You probably don't intend to screw that up.

If there is a listing of points to not flub, "your future" has to be high on the checklist.

Your choices lead to your destiny. Do you believe that? You should. It's true.

Eventually, what you do– as well as who you actually are– establishes what you ultimately achieve.

6. Realize your potential.

The wonderful thing about capacity is that it can build upon itself. If you can simply get the snowball rolling, the energy of movement will take control. Assume for a moment regarding the people you admire. Why do you admire them? You are probably attracted to them since they teem with understood possibility. When we see individuals exerting this sort of energy, it compels us to attract ourselves closer to them as well as to end up being a part of what they are doing.

So today you have a selection. Will you sit at the top of capital simply contemplating your capacities? Or will you give yourself a little push as well as barrel down that hillside, knocking over obstacles standing in your way?

7. Attract opportunity.

Opportunities and success are not something you pursue always but something you bring in by becoming an attractive individual.

If you can create your abilities, keep fine-tuning all the parts of your personality and also yourself, your health, your relationships so that you become an attractive individual– you'll draw opportunities.

8. Devote to living your desires.

Once you dedicate yourself to living your desires, the lids blinding your eyes will be lifted. A totally new globe will open to your sight.

You will certainly see chances that have actually remained in your reach the whole time, ones your mindful mind just did not attend to. The fundamental change happening is your self-identity. This is the defining moment.

When this change has actually occurred, your whole world adjusts. Absolutely nothing ends up being difficult to you. Your only restrictions are your consciousness, which is promptly broadening.

Whatever you desire swiftly becomes yours because you see what the majority of people don't. Since you can see it anywhere, you are running.

9. Never ever be pleased.

Even after you accomplish an objective, you're not material. For you, it's not also about the goal. It has to do with the climb to see just how far you can press on your own.

Does this make you ungrateful? Absolutely not. You're entirely humbled and also thankful for every little thing in your life, which is why you will never ever obtain complacent or lazy.

10. Add worth to others.

When you base on the coastline and enjoy the waves hitting the shore, do you assume there's any type of end to the water? There is, obviously, however we cannot comprehend it, so we believe salt water is endlessly abundant.

You would certainly never ever refute a bucketful to a youngster developing a sand castle because you can re-fill that container over and over again. That's just how the abundance state of mind works. You distribute appreciation, recognition, concepts, expertise and money because you understand there's plenty to go around.

What you distribute will certainly return to you a thousand times over.

11. Make the most of the infinite possibilities ahead of you.

Explore the one-of-a-kind, unlimited possibilities within you. Remember that when you service enhancing on your own, you're adding to the young people, vitality and elegance of your mind.

Different economic categories of society

Hopefully, by now you understand that money is simply an agreement about value, and that providing value is the only real road to riches. But the practical question remains, what paths can you follow to accumulate significant wealth?

The key to providing value over the long-run, and the point at which many people get confused, is that there are only a few basic strategies for accumulating wealth. There may be various combinations and a few exceptions (you might win the lottery!), but there are only a handful of ways to create or attract wealth.

The first method is through employment. This means getting a job with a good company, hopefully doing work you enjoy, and earning promotions and pay raises over time, until you are rewarded with various bonuses and a substantial paycheck.

In most countries, this is the most common and least efficient strategy for making money.

Income is taxed at very high levels, and taxes are deducted from your paycheck, so there is no chance to invest before the government takes its share.

There are very few jobs that pay enough after taxes to facilitate the accumulation of significant wealth. For most Americans (and citizens of other post-industrial nations), taxes on earned income are simply too high, and as you get the raises and bonuses, the percentage of income lost to taxation actually goes up, usually even faster than your raises. A "progressive" or graduated income tax is specifically designed and intended to do exactly that!

There will always be a few CEO's, movie stars, and others who are paid large salaries, but it's worth noting that the few people who are paid at that level usually insist that their salaries be paid as a "compensation package" that takes advantage of stock options, deferred income or other techniques for reducing income taxes.

Remember, employers must pay you less than your skills are worth. Employers rightly expect to make a profit on the capital, management skills, and risks they invested to create your job. Additionally, as we discussed previously, in the global economy, there will be more competition for the good-paying, high-value jobs that are available. As a result, both salaries and job security will go down as we enter the new century.

For most people, earned income (a job) is an inefficient way to provide value or accumulate wealth. While there are many reasons to work as an employee (security, convenience, mobility, etc.), making large sums of cash is not one of them.

The second path to financial independence is **Self-Employment.**

This is the choice of many professionals and home-based businesses. From an income perspective, there are two main advantages. As the self-employed owner of a small business (often called a "micro-business"), you can set your hourly rate, and you have some freedom to work when and if you choose. You can adjust your schedule and workload according to family responsibilities, your personal preferences and take a day off when you want to.

The government offers substantial tax advantages in exchange for the risks you take in creating your own job. As your own boss, you are responsible for your own office, your tools, marketing, management, billing and production. The government recognizes that this represents substantial risk (most new businesses ultimately fail), and it represents lots of hard work. As your "partner" the government expects to be paid (in taxes), but will cooperate with you in permitting some accounting and tax benefits.

The down-side is that, while we refer to it as a business, in fact, it is usually still a job. For most self-employed people, their income stops the moment they get sick, take time off, or retire. And, many people find that being both the boss, and the most important employee, is very stressful.

As a self-employed professional, with perhaps a small number of employees working for you, the bulk of the responsibility is on your shoulders. If you take a leave of absence or are not able to do your work as an attorney, accountant, sales person or graphic designer, your income usually stops. "No work, no pay" is the rule, and very few self-employed professionals ever move past this level.

Many independent contractors, artists, multi-level marketing professionals and other small office, home-office businesses are in this category. Freedom and independence are wonderful, but it is a hard path to financial wealth.

The third path to financial independence is **business ownership.** This is a much rarer and riskier, but potentially more rewarding path to wealth.

Businesses are systems that deliver value by organizing and combining the efforts of many people. Creating a business requires leadership, organizational and management skills, and capital. It means taking risks, and reaping the rewards if things work out.

Restaurants are great examples of systems that multiply effort, create jobs, and create wealth.

Going back to McDonalds, the system delivers burgers, and makes money whether the owner is present or not. Most self-made millionaires are business owners.

There are many disadvantages and difficulties in starting a business, particularly compared to the simplicity of having your own company as a self-employed professional. (Remember this distinction: all businesses are organized as a "company", but not every "company" is run as a business!) Starting or running a business requires great skill at understanding and managing people, inventory, cash flow, and sales. As a business, you'll have employees to hire, train, supervise and sometimes, fire. There are legal and accounting complexities and you'll need talented (and expensive) professionals to advise you.

But, the huge advantage of owning a business is that the system, if it is designed and managed appropriately, can largely "run itself". The owner of a well-run restaurant does not have to be physically present every moment the restaurant is open for business. The owner of a manufacturing plant does not personally box and ship every widget that goes out the door.

Once a business is running smoothly, it creates value (and cash) indefinitely. The critical value-added component of a business is rarely the product or service it produces directly, but rather the value of the jobs it creates and the business's ability to organize and focus effort to get a specific result.

To take an extreme example, Microsoft is generally acknowledged to be among the most successful businesses in modern history. But the little CD's they sell have almost no intrinsic value. In fact, the cost of producing CD's is so low that many companies give them away as advertising freebies. Bill Gates' genius is in organizing a diverse army of programmers, engineers, visionary thinkers, shipping clerks, lawyers, janitors and advertising executives to produce and deliver thousands of CD's that contain code to make our computers work.

The company is immensely profitable because it has been able to organize the talents of many different people. By bringing the contributions of different people together, Microsoft produces value-added software that has made Mr. Gates, and thousands of his employees and stock-holders, rich.

Starting, organizing and running a business is one of the most reliable paths to wealth. There are tax incentives, and if things turn out well, it can create a stream of cash that lasts for generations.

It is interesting to note that for over 200 years in America, immigrants have been among the greatest beneficiaries of this pattern. Whether it was the Irish or the Italians or the Eastern Europeans of the 19th century, or more recent immigrants from Asia and Latin America, immigrants have traditionally arrived poor, and they have suffered from discrimination.

Many don't speak English, and they are often prohibited from entering the professions or other high-skill, high-salary jobs. So, what do they do?

They open family-owned businesses. They become florists or landscapers or dry cleaners.

They own the local gas station or the janitorial service that cleans our homes and office buildings. Families will often pool their capital to buy a taxi or, especially in New York, to buy a push-cart and sell hot-dogs or pizza or deli sandwiches. With the profits, they buy another cart, and then another, until within a generation, the family becomes an "overnight success"!

Business ownership is clearly not for everyone, but it is one of the most reliable paths to wealth.

The only other path to wealth is **investing**, or using your money in ways that create value and wealth over time. The classic American investments have been land and buildings, stocks and bonds, and precious metals or other commodities.

The key to creating wealth through investing is that you are permitting other people to use your money (your accumulated and easily transferable value) to create businesses of their own. In return for the use of your money, you share the wealth created by their business.

In the case of investing in an office building, for instance, you use your money to create a physical location where other people can conduct business. In exchange for your investment in the property, they pay you "rent", which is really a part of the proceeds from the business they transact inside the building.

If you buy stock in a company, or loan its money in the form of bonds, the relationship is even more specific. The managers of the business take your money (and pool it with money from many other investors) and add their organizational and leadership abilities to create a business. If there are profits, you are entitled to share in the proceeds.

Non-investors often think investing is an easy way to make money, but that it requires lots of cash to get started. In my opinion, the reverse is true. You can begin investing for less than $1000, but it does take skill, knowledge and discipline to understand great investments. Many beginning "investors" are really gamblers, and like gamblers, they eventually lose everything.

Serious investing is not gambling or a matter of luck. Skilled investors educate themselves about the property, stocks, or other ventures they are considering for investment. They read, compare one investment with another, and seek expert advice. Often, the best way for new investors to start out is through mutual funds, which is a form of investing where the risk (and later, the profits) are shared among many investors, and the investments are managed by a professional.

Gamblers, who would never go near a poker game or bet on a horse-race, will nevertheless, bet on a "hot tip" about a stock, or rush to buy shares of the latest miracle story on Wall Street.

That is not investing!

Investing is a carefully considered decision to invest your accumulated skills, effort and abilities in a specific business venture, in the form of cash. Over the years, I've observed that the investors who make the most money, those who routinely get returns of 50% to several hundred percent on their money year after year, are very cautious. They read and study investing, and they learn from both their own mistakes and by observing the wins (and the losses) of other skilled investors.

Investors like Donald Trump, don't gamble. They build casinos where other people gamble. Important distinction!

Throughout history, investing in land and buildings, stocks and bonds, or commodities, has been a reliable and efficient way to accumulate wealth. Much like owning your own business, the government has traditionally created tax advantages of various kinds to reward investors for the risks they take. "Capital gains" taxes, which are much lower than income taxes, and various credits and incentives for specific types of investments are a few examples.

It's often been said that the poor and middle-class work for money; the wealthy have their money work for them. That's a cliché, but like most clichés, there is great truth in it. This is a reminder that investing is complex and there are risks.

Even highly skilled investors occasionally get an unpleasant surprise. Consult with experts and develop your skills through practice and education. However, to accumulate great wealth, do invest! Learn the skills and practice until you gain confidence. Start small if that's appropriate in your situation, but do let your money work for you.

The 20% Solution

This chapter is about a technique that will allow anyone – yes, I said anyone – to accumulate substantial wealth.

That's a huge promise, but I believe I can fulfill it because the laws of mathematics are on my side. Albert Einstein observed that "Compound interest is the 8th wonder of the world." The plan is based on having compound interest working for you, rather than against you.

So, how do you get rich?

Very simple: Save 20% of everything you make, invest for the long haul, and you will retire rich. Period. The math makes it a sure thing.

From Biblical time's right up through recent books like "The Wealthy Barber", many people have advised, "Save 10% for the future". For thousands of years, the vast majority have complained that they "can't afford to", and believing their own complaints and doubts, they never do. Predictably, since they never start, they never accumulate any money!

Some people question whether they can actually save 20%, and others ask whether it is figured before or after taxes. To an amazing degree – if you get a calculator and do the math – it really doesn't matter. And, if you can't start with 10%, start with 7% or even less. But: start!

The key is consistency and perseverance over time. If you save only $3000 per year, in monthly deposits of $250 each, in 30 years at 12% interest, you will have over $882,000! If you start early, and have the discipline and the desire, almost every average, economically middle-class individual should expect to be a millionaire before they retire. Unfortunately, of course, we know that most will not only fail to retire wealthy, but will in fact, be quite poor. That is unacceptable!

So, how can you find and save 20%? Easy! Here are a couple suggestions:

First, figure out how folks who make just a little bit less than you do survive! In your neighborhood there are people who make slightly less than you do. They are still alive!

They have food and clothing, a roof over their heads, and shoes on their feet. Now, they may not have new shoes, or a fancy car, and maybe they don't eat out as often as you do, but they do survive! **That's critical.**

To pay off your debts or to increase your savings, you are going to have to spend less each month. We've talked about increasing income, and that is an option. But, over and over again (we all know this story), as income goes up, spending goes up just a tiny bit faster!

Making more money will not make you rich!

Spending less will!

Second, pay yourself first. That old advice simply means that before you pay any other bills, even the mortgage, you put money in savings first! There's a simple logic to this.

No one will remind you or pressure you or encourage you to save. You must do that on your own, as an act of self-discipline and personal pride. But you can depend on lots of people to remind you to pay all your other bills. Trust me on this!

If you forget to pay the phone company, they will remind you! They'll send you a note, they might even call you up to remind you. They are very helpful that way! You know what?

Everyone else you owe is just as helpful! The garbage collector, your landlord, even the nice people at VISA will remind you to pay them, if you forget. But none of them, not a single one, will ever advise you to pay yourself.

To save and invest 20% for your future, spend a bit less, and pay yourself first. And, it should go without saying, but I'll mention it anyway: once you put the money in savings, it never –never – comes back out! That is for retirement. It is to pass on to your children, and their children, and their children after that.

If you want to save for a vacation or a new car or your kids college, that is in addition to the 20%. It has to be! Again, watch the logic. If you save, and then spend it all, what's the point? Save 20% of everything you make and be very, very reluctant to ever take it back out!

If you save 20%, within a very short period of time you'll have to make some decisions about where to invest it. There are many books, magazines and planners you can consult, but my personal advice is always to start by paying off your debts.

Depending on your tax bracket, the "after tax, real rate of return" of paying off an 18% credit card debt can be as high as a 30% annual rate of return! You won't get that good a return anywhere else! Pay off your debts!

Then, invest in the stock market through mutual funds. I respect that many people have other opinions, but for most folks, a good, solid, boring mutual fund is the golden path to riches.

Yes, you should invest in tax-sheltered retirement plans first; yes, there are other investment possibilities; yes, the market can go down. But to retire wealthy, pick a great, long-term growth fund, invest regularly, and watch the system work for you.

I am convinced the biggest hurdle that stops folks from getting rich is: They never get started! Pay off your debts, start saving, and don't try to get rich quick. In this instance, boring is good!

Mutual Funds: The best way to start

Everyone who follows the financial news has heard of mutual funds and knows the stock market has seen a lot of ups and downs over the past few years, but overall, there has been a steady growth. In fact, by most measures, the stock market has made more people more money, and done it more reliably, than any other investment over the past 75 years! If you want to accumulate substantial wealth, you must include stocks in your investments!

Most people who "invest" don't study the market. They don't understand it, and they don't have time to manage their portfolio wisely. That's where mutual funds come in. I respect that other people have other opinions, and certainly not all mutual funds are well managed – you MUST choose wisely and use appropriate caution! But, for most folks, a good, solid, boring mutual fund is the golden path to riches.

Here are my Top 10 reasons to invest in mutual funds:

1. Selection. You can select from thousands of funds (you'll find one to suit your needs) and you can get information on them easily. Magazines like "Money" are easy to find.

Most credit unions have information, and your local library is a goldmine – and there's the Internet.

2. Start Small. Most mutual funds will let you start with less than $1000, and if you set it up for automatic deposits, some will let you start with only $50. I've spent more than that in a restaurant!

3. Simplicity. You deposit 10% of your income every month. Just pay yourself first, then pay the mortgage, then pay everyone else.

4. Professional management. I don't always have time to research, select, and monitor individual stocks. So, I pay a professional a small fee to do it for me. A good fund manager will make you rich! Plus, lately a lot of wealth management and investments solutions have surfaced on the internet and in the form of apps that make investing so easy and convenient especially for the millennials.

5. Compound interest. Depending on what index you pick, the U.S. stock market has gone up an average of over 12% per year for the past 10 years, and it's been almost that high for the past 20 years. The market fluctuates, but the beauty of this is, you don't care!

Over 10, 20, or 30 years, the system works!

6. Dollar-cost-averaging. The details are complicated, but by investing every single month, whether the market is up or down, you get a tremendous boost from mathematics.

Your "average cost" will always be less than the "average price" you paid! That is money in your pocket!

7. Diversification. A broad-based growth fund typically invests in dozens of companies in different industries, sometimes even in different countries around the world. If one stock goes down, hopefully dozens of others will go up. There is excellent protection and sound risk management built-in to these funds.

8. Specialization. If you prefer, and if you do the research, there are funds that invest in only a very small number of companies. If you can accept the additional risk, you can invest in one particular industry, or one country, or in companies with certain management styles. This creates the potential for even greater profits if you select the right industry, but be aware it also brings greater potential risk.

9. Fund "Families". Most mutual funds are offered by management companies that sponsor several different funds, with different objectives. They make it easy to move your money between funds, so as your goals change, you can adjust your investments with a quick phone call, or on the Internet.

10. Momentum. Once you get started, your enthusiasm builds. Once you have money "in the market", you'll track it, manage it, and in all probability, your desire to save will increase. If you've had difficulty saving in the past…start now! Those monthly statements will be positive reminders to do even more.

There are risks and there can be costs to investing in mutual funds, so be sure you read the prospectus and understand the details before you invest. The stock market does fluctuate, and I strongly advise you to read several books and consult a professional if this is all new for you. For almost everyone, regular deposits to a long-term growth mutual fund is the sure, simple and reliable way to get rich! But you must: start!

Keys to Keeping What You Have

There are a lot of resources on the best ways to protect what you have or shelter it from taxes, or hide it from nosy neighbors. Nevertheless, now we'll be covering the more routine, every-day things that impact almost all of us. If you need specialized information on how to hide your wealth overseas, I'm afraid you'll need to look elsewhere.

Most of us lose what we make in one of four basic ways:

1. The "leaky bucket"

2. We pay too much in taxes

3. We fail to insure and protect what we have

4. We don't have an appropriate Will or Living Trust

#1: The Leaky Bucket

Almost all of us spend more in cash and with credit cards than we imagine. One of the challenges I give many of my clients is to track every single purchase for just one month.

Keep a notebook, and just for a short time, try to track every single dollar you spend. When they do that, almost without fail my clients call to tell me they are astonished, appalled and even ashamed at how much money "disappears" each month.

If you spend just $5 per day on lunch, that's over $100 per month. If you buy a couple cans of pop, or stop for ice cream, or maybe bring pizza home for dinner once in a while, it's not uncommon to have those small, every-day purchases total over $500 per month! Even an inexpensive dinner out, followed by a movie and maybe a drink on the way home can easily total over $100 for a couple. Take the kids, and Saturday afternoon at the movies can shrink your wallet in a hurry!

Now, none of these are bad things. I enjoy dinner in a nice restaurant or a movie as much as anyone. But, if you want to control your finances, you must add these things up, tell the truth about how much they cost, and make some decisions about how many of them you can afford.

It may help to realize that all of these things are purchased with after-tax dollars. That means that a $10 pizza actually costs you about $18 in time and effort, about $8 for the government, with $10 left for the pizza guy. Multiply that by the cost of a weekend at that nice resort, or the price of a luxury car, and pretty soon you're talking about real money!

One of the observations Thomas Stanley makes in "The Millionaire Next Door" is that wealthy people are very cautious about spending money. Most

171

do not own expensive watches, fancy cars or expensive suits. Those things simply cost too much for a rich person to afford them!

Here are some simple suggestions that can save you hundreds of dollars per year:

- Keep a simple notebook and record every purchase. Keep it simple, but tracking your daily purchases will almost certainly help you spend less, and spend more wisely.
- Rent movies, make popcorn at home. Obviously, just one example, but simplify!
- Healthy snacks and simple meals often cost less and take less time than commercial counterparts. Eating an apple instead of a candy bar saves in many ways.
- Use coupons and shop when things are on sale. Always shop from a list, and never go to the grocery store when you're hungry!
- Comparison shop for insurance. You might easily save $100 per year on car insurance. Installing smoke detectors is smart, and will save on home-owners insurance.
- Controversial, but consider driving an older, smaller or cheaper car. Annual costs for vehicles and transportation are typically far greater than most people realize.
- Greatly reduce credit card spending, unless you are one of the few with the discipline to use them wisely, buy little, and pay off your balance every month.
- The examples are endless, but the point is the same. Don't spend money you don't have to!

2: We Pay Too Much in Taxes

Most of the people, particularly those who work for a paycheck, pay the bulk of all the taxes.

That may not be fair, but it's the way the system is designed. To reduce your taxes and put more money in your pocket, become educated about the tax laws and learn to use them to your advantage.

Begin by learning the distinction between tax avoidance, and tax evasion. Tax evasion is illegal and stupid. You'll eventually be audited, get caught and have a world of headaches.

Even before that, you'll have the anxiety of knowing you've cheated. Don't do it!

Tax avoidance on the contrary is not only legal, it's recognized by the Courts as smart and ethical business. To reduce your taxes, consider the following steps:

- Always – always! – fund any tax-sheltered or tax-deferred investments first.

Fund your 401-k or any equivalent schemes, and other tax advantaged accounts.

- Look for ways to reduce your personal property tax. Often appealing the assessment on your home can result in substantial savings, now and for every year to come.
- Understand the benefits of capital gains taxes, and invest for the long haul.
- Understand tax laws relating to certain types of real-estate and bond investments. The interest on many municipal bonds is partially or entirely tax free! Look into it.

#3: Insurance

I recently read that the odds are 1 in 4 that a healthy adult will be disabled for a year, sometime during their working life. That's an amazing statistic! Yet, disability income insurance is one of the least understood and least appreciated forms of insurance. While you're healthy, contact your local agent and find out about guaranteeing your income if you become injured or suffer a lengthy illness.

Beyond that, most Americans do not have the correct type or amount of life insurance.

Almost everyone has either too little, or too much. If you are single and have no children, why do you need life insurance? But if you have small children, a new house and a pile of bills (who can afford life insurance?) you really, really need to protect those you love.

Consult with at least 2 different independent insurance agents, and get solid advice. You should have appropriate insurance on:

- Your home and your belongings
- Your car
- Your life and your health
- Your income and earning capability
- Your business assets, including intellectual property rights

Again, read Consumer Reports and other magazines. Become informed. I strongly recommend Suze Orman's book, "The 9 Steps to Financial Freedom", listed in the appendix.

You can often save hundreds, even thousands of dollars by shopping around and buying the right insurance. But never try to save a nickel by not having insurance you need to protect yourself, your loved ones and your future.

#4: Have a Will and a Living Will

There has been much written in recent years about various forms of trusts and other forms of estate planning, so the term "will" in the title of this section is used generically to indicate that you have taken responsible, thoughtful steps to pass on your wealth when you die.

The fact is, every citizen does have a will, whether you know it or not. The state has written one for you. It's clumsy, impersonal, and almost certainly does not suit your unique situation, but it is right there, in the legal code. If you die without having written your own will, that's OK – the Courts will simply use the one the government wrote for you. Is that what you want? I doubt it!

Even a complex estate can often be handled with a simple will costing less than $500 and taking no more than a couple of hours to prepare. Is a basic will adequate and complete in your situation? Maybe not, but it's a start, and it's a whole lot better than nothing. Get started!

Here are just a few things to consider:

- If you have substantial assets, you will want to consider a trust or some legal way to transfer wealth to your loved ones before you die. Estate taxes can run as high as 80%. I consider that obscene, but it's the law!
- Decide in advance who should receive the bulk of your estate, and be very specific about the details. Maybe one of your children should receive a particular family heirloom, while another should receive stock in your company. Spell it out!

- Consider the ramifications if you and your spouse should both die, perhaps in an accident or other disaster. Who should receive your estate then? Who will care for your children?
- Decide if you want to leave something to your favorite charity, house of worship, or educational institution. There are very important tax advantages to setting this up ahead of time. Your attorney can advise you about the details.

Finally, a note about "Living Wills". The odds are that you will not be hit by lightning or die instantly in an accident. Most probably, you will grow old, get sick, and for at least a short time, you will be unable to participate in decisions about your own health care. That's when a living will be invaluable. Tell your loved ones what you want! Indicate if you wish to be an organ donor. Decide now, while you are healthy, what measures you want (or do not want) taken to keep you alive. Decide now, and write it down!

Most self-made millionaires have neither a large income, nor a flashy life-style; but they do hang on to what they earn, and they use it wisely. Paying attention to the costs of your lifestyle, and simplifying where you can, makes a huge difference. There are often non-financial benefits that turn out to be even more important. An entire movement, often referred to as the "Voluntary Simplicity" movement has discovered the joys of being home more, working less, spending less and throwing away less. Often, by reducing expenses we add not only to our bank accounts, but to the quality of our lives.

Route to become a millionaire

There is perhaps no more important decision than to take charge of your own financial future.

We live in a world of opportunity, and yet most Americans are buried in credit card and other debt. We are surrounded by people who are getting rich, but most of us are running in place.

If you can read this, you are literate, have a computer, you are part of the "wired generation".

You can become as financially independent as you wish to be. Here are the Top 10 keys to your financial success:

THE MILLIONAIRE'S WAY

1. Decide to be financially successful.

This is different from wishing, hoping, wanting or even desiring to be rich. Make a commitment that this is going to happen! Financial independence is not an accident or matter of luck, and it usually requires some inconvenience. Have you decided to achieve this goal?

2. Understand how money works.

Most of us never studied finance or investing in school.

Most of us were never even taught to balance a checkbook! To master anything, you have to understand it. Read. Study what successful people do. Take classes.

3. Master your relationship with money.

Some of us spend for excitement, to show off, to prove we can. Some of us are addicted to spending, and some of us are just careless about it.

Whatever your relationship with money, understand it and develop a relationship of respect, appreciation and gratitude. Use it wisely!

4. Set specific goals.

They should be challenging, but not unbelievable, just out of reach but not out of sight. Challenge yourself to be out of debt by a specific date. Make a commitment to saving an exact amount each month.

5. Develop a budget.

A budget is a set of dreams and aspirations. It is how you really, really want to use money to benefit your family and run your life. Budget to buy the things you really want, and to eliminate the "impulses", the toys that waste too much of our income. A budget is a map to your destination. Have one and use it!

6. Reduce spending.

Yes, this comes after making a budget, because when you begin getting control of your money (rather than the other way around) you have powerful new reasons to reduce expenses. Most self-made millionaires live far below their means! You should too.

7. Begin investing.

Most of us spend or speculate. Both are roads to disaster! Invest in things you understand. Invest cautiously, wisely, and regularly. The objective is not to "make a killing", but to get rich over time. Know and obey the distinction between gambling, and putting your money to work for you.

8. Increase assets.

Most people try to increase their income, and that's a mistake. Making more money means paying more taxes. It takes time and hard work, and when wealth arrives in the form of cash, it's easier to spend. Millionaires buy stocks and buildings; they invest in assets that will make them rich – and that are hard to spend on a whim!

9. Reduce taxes.

A lot of folks pay more in taxes than for food, clothing and shelter combined! It is your largest expense! The poor and middle class don't realize how much they pay because it's deducted from their pay check. The wealthy know there are legal and appropriate ways to shelter income, to invest in socially-responsible ways, and that the tax code encourages this. Learn the tax laws and use them for your benefit! (Yes, it's the most boring reading you'll ever do, and worth it!)

10. Use your wealth wisely.

Someone once said, "The reason most of us aren't rich is that we'd spend it all on ourselves." Give. Share. Help others. When you use money to make a difference, to have a positive impact, you get the chance to do more. Being greedy and selfish will not draw money to you. Investing in your community, will!

To begin your education about money and becoming a millionaire, I highly recommend several books on the subject. Two of the best are: "The Millionaire Next Door" by Thomas Stanley and William Danko, and "Rich Dad, Poor Dad" by Robert Kiyosaki and Sharon Lechter.

Most middle-class Americans will earn well over a million dollars during their working lives.

Even if you start working as late as age 30 (after college and a few years of kicking around looking for your niche) and plan to retire a few years early, say at age 55, and assume your average income is $50,000 per year, during those twenty-five years you will earn 1.25 million dollars! With the combined earnings of husband and wife, and perhaps having started work at a younger age or being willing to continue into your 60's, the potential to earn (and pay taxes) on several million dollars is very real.

Where does the money go? That is entirely up to you! As many observers have noted, millionaires don't necessarily earn more, but they spend less. They live below their means.

They live well, but they do not spend on items that depreciate, or on frivolous items to impress their friends. They invest wisely, often in their own businesses, or in stocks or other investments that they understand and are willing to monitor closely. They take money seriously, and they expect to retire wealthy. They value money, and they pay attention to it.

They manage it, accumulate it and let it work for them, rather than always working for money, from one paycheck to the next.

The secret to becoming a millionaire? Do what millionaires do, and do it over and over, until you arrive at your goal.

The way ahead

If you've read this far, you are obviously ready to take control of your finances, invest wisely and accumulate substantial wealth. We've talked at great length about what money represents and how it works. We've talked about the various paths to accumulating wealth, and the advantages of mutual funds. We've talked about taxes and where money tends to "evaporate".

Now it's time to review the comments in the introduction about this being a "Declaration of Financial Independence" and a call to action. Like many other books on money and investing, much of what we've covered is understandable. In fact, I hope much of what you've read has been familiar, as if you're being reminded of things you already knew.

The greatest secret of accumulating wealth is this: It is not a secret!

There are books on it. People will show you and teach you how. They will coach you; they will respect and admire and encourage you. They will hire you to manage their business and show you the ropes. They will sell you a franchise or an apartment building. Shares of stock and mutual funds are for sale at your local bank, and there are money managers, investment professionals and financial advisors in every community who are honest and who will work hard to help you become rich. Most of us know this.

We still get caught up in daily life. Just as Madison Avenue intends, we are tempted by the advertising, by our children's "need" for the latest clothes, toys and gadgets. We "need" a new car or deserve a vacation, so we pull out a credit card or write a check. Next month, we are in the same financial spot we were in the month before. We have all done this.

So, it doesn't surprise me that much of what you have read sounded familiar. You've heard it (or something similar) before. Like so many other books on money and investing, you can easily set this down, pat yourself on the back for how much you know and how smart you are, and take no action! If that happens, I have wasted my time in writing this, and you have wasted your time reading it.

Information without action is worthless! I can tell you that if you are not satisfied with your current financial situation, and if you want a different result in the years ahead, you must take action!

Now, I do not know what the most important next step is for you. Everyone who reads this will be in a different place, with different values and different financial responsibilities. Based on the statistics of where most Americans are, I can make some guesses. The list on the next page starts at the very beginning. If you have already taken care of the basics, great!

Congratulate yourself, and keep reading down the list until you find the steps that fit your situation. Check them off, and get to work!

Here are my suggestions for key action steps:

Action Step	If this step is completed, check it off. If not, write the words, "Do This!" and put a date by which you will complete this step.
Balance my checkbook, add up the bills and figure out where I stand financially.	
Accurately list my monthly income and expenses.	
Establish a written plan – a budget – for how I want to use my money each month.	
Commit to saving 10% of my income every single month.	
Commit to paying off all consumer and credit card debt.	
Review and be certain I am living below my means, every month.	
Create a long-term plan for my financial future and take active responsibility for making certain I reach my goals.	

Read one book or magazine on money and investing every month. Become the best educated person I know about money and creating wealth.	
Have my "Performance Team" in place, including at least: an attorney, accountant, financial advisor, and insurance agent I know and trust.	
Use my knowledge and skill, and the advice of my Team, to invest in things I understand and can monitor over time	

In the end, it's not about the money. It never is.

As we studied in the beginning, money is simply a convenient way to measure and transfer value. Money is a number that represents your contribution, your effort and your skill. If you collect lots of it, and put it under your mattress or bury it in your backyard, I would argue that both financially and personally, you have truly wasted your life. Yes, you might buy nice toys, a big house, or take some fancy trips around the world, but of what use is that?

Life is meant to be invested. Our lives are meant to create value, to make a difference. I want to cast a long shadow, to leave footprints in the sand where I have walked. I want to be remembered, and to do that, I must contribute to my community.

There are as many ways to contribute as there are people. Your talents and interests are unique, and I would never try to tell another person the "right" way for them to participate in our community. Some will create jobs or build homes and apartments; others contribute to charitable foundations or create educational scholarships. Some, like President Carter, retire early and spend

20 years building homes for Habitat for Humanity. Others mentor children, or invest in struggling young businesses to help them grow.

Whatever is right for you, find a way to make a difference.

Whether you refer to it as God or the Universe or just as Life, there is something that does not want you to be poor. You need not be poor in spirit, poor in opportunity, or poor in finances.

We will not all control vast fortunes, but we all have the ability, and the response-ability, to accumulate wealth. Having done so, we have the obligation to use it wisely and do something magnificent with it!

What will you do with your fortune? Take time to figure it out and cherish all the thoughts!

Until then,

Prriya Kaur

"The gratification of wealth is not found in mere possession or in lavish expenditure but in its wise application."

– Miguel de Cervantes

Some heads up for the next day: *Tomorrow we'll be reaching the last leg of our journey and we're going to conclude everything by finding the true meaning of life – staying happy!*

The surprise/Bonus Day

Finding the true happiness

The real meaning of happiness and rejoicing upon its essence in different aspects of life

BEFORE STARTING OFF WITH TODAY

● **Take a while to go through the Self-image Reformulation exercise from day one.**

● **Go through this daily affirmation:**

I am born to succeed, the infinite within me cannot fail. The divine law and order govern my life, divine peace fill my soul, and divine love saturates my mind.

Infinite intelligence guides me in all ways, God's riches flow to me freely. I am advancing, moving forward and growing mentally, spiritually, financially and in other ways.

I know these truths are sinking into my subconscious mind and will grow after their kind, today is God's Day. I chose happiness, success, prosperity and peace of mind,

All I need is within me.

1. Recall your purpose of life, ambitions and goals from day four.

2. Revisit the section of PRACTICING THE LAW OF ATTRACTION FOR WEALTH MANIFESTATION IN A DIFFERENT WAY and focus upon the third point '**Alter your mindset**' by visualizing your wealth abundance:

What would your life be like if you finally get the desired amount of wealth? What would it take to be in such a position? Feel all the goodness, imagine yourself being happy and cherish all the positivity.

How would your house be? What lifestyle changes would happen in your day-to-day life? Now think about the people around you. What impact would you be making in their lives? Feel all your valuable possessions around you, the things that you always wanted in life.

To finish programming your mind, imagine yourself containing a vast amount of knowledge and experience within you, and you're finally living the life you've always wanted. You are content and ready to take anything that comes your way!

Once upon a time there lived a very rich and wealthy man in a big city. He led a luxurious life. He always boasted about his wealth to his friends and relatives. His son was studying in a distant city and returned home for holiday. The rich man wanted to show his son how rich he was, but his son wasn't interested in any luxurious lifestyles.

However, the man wanted to make his son realize that his lifestyle was extremely rich and that the poor people suffered a lot. So, he planned a day's visit to the entire town.

The father and son took a chariot and visited the entire town. They returned home in two days. The father was happy that his son was quiet after seeing the poor people suffering. So, he asked, "Dear son, how was the trip? Did you enjoy it?" "Yes dad. It was lovely," replied the son. Then he asked him what he had learnt from the trip. The son was silent. The father said that he was happy that his son had realized how the poor people actually lived and suffered. "No", replied the son.

Then he said, "We have two dogs, they have ten. We have a big pool in our garden, but they have a massive bay with no end! We have expensive lights, but they have endless stars to light their nights. We have a house on a small piece of land, but they have abundant fields that go beyond the horizon.

We are protected by huge walls, but they surround themselves with each other. We have to buy food, but they are so rich that they can cultivate their own.

The father was stunned and speechless on hearing his son's words.

Finally, the son said, "Thank you, father, for showing me who is rich and who is poor."

All about being Happy

What is happiness? It seems like an odd and clichéd question being put up yet again, but is it? Do you know how to define happiness? Do you think happiness is the same thing to you as it is to others?

In fact, happiness has a pretty important role in our lives, and it can have a huge impact on the way we live our lives. Although researchers are yet to pin down the definition or an agreed-upon framework for happiness, there's a lot we have learned in the last few decades.

But what's the point of it all? Does it even make a difference in our lives?

Today as we'll be concluding our journey, we're going to discover the science of happiness, what it actually is, and why it matters.

Our creative, science-based approach will help you learn more about your values and goals and will give you the tools to inspire a sense of meaning and happiness in your life and the lives of people around you.

However unselfish we may think our actions to be, they are still all motivated by our desire for our own happiness. Even if we sacrifice our time, our money, our comforts and conveniences, or anything else that is precious to us, in order to do some altruistic action, whether to help some other person or to support some noble cause, the ultimate driving force behind such sacrifice is our desire to be happy. We do altruistic actions only because doing so makes us feel happy. Let's take a look at the definition of happiness so that we're all on the same page. A typical Dictionary's definition of "happiness" is a simple one: "The state of being happy."

Not exactly what we are looking for, isn't it? Perhaps we need to dive a little deeper. If we extend the definition a little bit, it'd become more helpful to understand: "Feeling or showing pleasure or contentment."

That's better! So, happiness is the state of feeling or showing pleasure or contentment. From this definition, we can glean a few important points about happiness:

- Happiness is a state, not a trait; in other words, it isn't a long-lasting, permanent feature or personality trait, but a more fleeting, changeable state.

- Happiness is equated with feeling pleasure or contentment, meaning that happiness is not to be confused with joy, ecstasy, bliss, or other more intense feelings.
- Happiness can be either feeling or showing, which means that happiness is not necessarily an internal or external experience, but can be both.

Now we have a better grasp on what happiness is or at least, how we tend to frame it in our day to day lives. However, this definition is not the end-all, be-all definition. In fact, the debates around the true meaning of happiness are not yet the "settled" ones.

It isn't what you have, or who you are, or where you are, or what you are doing that makes you happy or unhappy. It is what you think about.

– Dale Carnegie

The meaning of happiness in Positive Psychology really depends on who you ask.

Happiness is often known by another name in positive psychology research: subjective wellbeing, or SWB. Some believe happiness is one of the core components of SWB, while others believe happiness is SWB. Regardless, you'll frequently find SWB used as a shorthand for happiness in the literature.

Speaking of the literature, you will find references to SWB everywhere. A quick Google search for the word "happiness" offers over 2 million results. Further, a scan for the same term in two of psychology's biggest online databases (PsycINFO and PsycARTICLES) returns thousands of results from academic and other journals, books, dissertations, and more.

With so many takes on happiness, it's no wonder that happiness is a little difficult to define scientifically; there is certainly disagreement about what, exactly, happiness is.

According to researchers Chu Kim-Prieto, Ed Diener, and their colleagues (2005), there are three main ways that happiness has been approached in positive psychology:

- Happiness as a global assessment of life and all its facets;

- Happiness as a recollection of past emotional experiences;
- Happiness as an aggregation of multiple emotional reactions across time.

Although they generally all agree on what happiness feels like, being satisfied with life, in a good mood, feeling positive emotions, feeling enjoyment, etc. researchers have found it difficult to agree on the scope of happiness.

However, for our purposes in this piece, it's enough to work off of a basic definition that melds the OED's definition with that of positive psychologists: happiness is a state characterized by contentment and general satisfaction with one's current situation.

The Science behind Happiness

Pleasure and Happiness

With close ties between pleasure and happiness, you might be wondering how to differentiate between them. After all, the OED definition of happiness describes it as a state of feeling pleasure!

The association between the two makes sense, and it's common to hear the two words used interchangeably outside of the literature; however, when it comes to the science of positive psychology, it is important to make a distinction between the two.

Happiness, as we described above, is a state characterized by feelings of contentment and satisfaction with one's life or current situation. On the other hand, pleasure is a more visceral, in-the-moment experience. It often refers to the sensory-based feelings we get from experiences like eating good food, getting a massage, receiving a compliment, or having sex.

Happiness, while not a permanent state, is a more stable state than pleasure. Happiness generally sticks around for longer than a few moments at a time, whereas pleasure can come and go in seconds.

Pleasure can contribute to happiness, and happiness can enhance or deepen feelings of pleasure, but the two can also be completely mutually exclusive. For example, you can feel a sense of happiness based on meaning and engagement that has nothing to do with pleasure, or you could feel pleasure but also struggle with guilt because of it, keeping you from feeling happy at the same time.

Happiness vs. meaning

Happiness and meaning have an even more distinct line between the two. Rarely are happiness and meaning confused or used interchangeably, and for a good reason they describe two very different experiences.

Unlike happiness, meaning is not a fleeting state that drifts throughout the day; it's a more comprehensive sense of purpose and feeling of contributing to something greater than yourself.

Humans may resemble many other creatures while striving for happiness, but the quest for meaning is a key part of what makes us human, and uniquely so.

- Roy Baumeister

As the quote from Baumeister and colleagues (2013) suggests, there are important distinctions between the methods of searching for and the benefits of experiencing happiness and meaning. Scott Barry Kaufman at Scientific American (2016) outlines these distinctions that Baumeister and his fellow researchers found between the two:

- Finding one's life easy or difficult was related to happiness, but not meaning;
- Feeling healthy was related to happiness, but not meaning;
- Feeling good was related to happiness, but not meaning;
- Scarcity of money reduced happiness more than meaning;
- People with more meaningful lives agreed that "relationships are more important than achievements;"
- Helping people in need was linked to meaning but not happiness;
- Expecting to do a lot of deep thinking was positively related to meaningfulness, but negatively with happiness;
- Happiness was related more to being a taker rather than a giver, whereas meaning was related more to being a giver than a taker;

- The more people felt their activities were consistent with the core themes and values of their self, the greater meaning they reported in their activities;
- Seeing oneself as wise, creative, and even anxious were all linked to meaning but had no relationship (and in some cases, even showed a negative relationship) to happiness.

Now that we know what happiness is, let's dive a little deeper. What does psychology have to tell us about happiness?

There are many different theories of happiness, but they generally fall into one of two categories based on how they conceptualize happiness (or well-being):

1. Hedonic happiness/well-being is happiness conceptualized as experiencing more pleasure and less pain; it is composed of an affective component (high positive affect and low negative affect) and a cognitive component (satisfaction with one's life);

2. Eudaimonic happiness/well-being conceptualizes happiness as the result of the pursuit and attainment of life purpose, meaning, challenge, and personal growth; happiness is based on reaching one's full potential and operating at full functioning

Some theories see happiness as a by-product of other, more important pursuits in life, while others see happiness as the end-goal for humans. Some theories state that pursuing happiness is pointless (although pursuing other important experiences and feelings may contribute to greater happiness), and some assume that happiness can be purposefully increased or enhanced.

Although they differ on the specifics, these theories generally agree on a few points:

- It's good to be happy, and people like being happy;
- Happiness is neither a totally fleeting, momentary experience nor a stable, long-term trait;
- At least some portion of our happiness is set by our genetics, but the amount varies from about 10% to 50%;
- The pursuit and attainment of pleasure will rarely lead to happiness;
- There are many sources that contribute to or compose happiness

What does self-happiness mean?

Although the term is not used very often, "self-happiness" refers to a sense of happiness or satisfaction with one's self. It is often associated with self-confidence, self-esteem, and other concepts that marry "the self" with feeling content and happy.

In general, it means that you are pleased with yourself and your choices, and with the person that you are.

Taking together all the various theories and findings on happiness, we know that there are at least a few factors that are very important for overall happiness:

- Individual income;
- Labor market status;
- Physical health;
- Family;
- Social relationships;
- Moral values;
- Experience of positive emotions.

All of these factors can contribute to a happy life, but research has found that good relationships are a vital ingredient.

When we are happy in our most important relationships (usually our spouse or significant other, our children and/or our parents, other close family members, and our closest friends), we tend to be happier.

We have some control over how our relationships go, so that leads us to an interesting and important question: can we increase our own happiness?

Can individuals learn how to be happy?

The answer from numerous studies is a resounding YES, you CAN. learn how to be happier.

The degree to which you can increase your happiness will widely depend on which theory you subscribe to, but there are no credible theories that allow absolutely no room for individual improvement. To improve your overall happiness, the most effective method is to look at the list of sources above and work on enhancing the quality of your experiences in each one of them.

For example, you can work on getting a higher salary (although a higher salary will only work up to about $75,000 USD a year), improve your health, work on developing and maintaining high-quality relationships, and overall, find ways to incorporate more positive feelings into your daily life. This does assume basic access to safety as well as social equality. Now the obvious question that pops up is, given our definitions, what does a happy life look like?

Of course, what it looks like will depend on the individual—a happy life for one person may be another's nightmare!

However, there are a few examples that can display a wide range of lives that can be conducive to happiness:

1. A woman who lives alone, has excellent relationships with her nieces and nephews, gives to charity, and finds meaning in her work;

2. A man who is happily married with three healthy children and a relatively low-paying job;

3. A widow who enjoys regular visits with her children and grandchildren, along with volunteering for local charities;

4. A cancer patient who has a wonderful support system and finds meaning in helping others make it through chemotherapy;

5. A social worker who works 70-hour weeks with no overtime pay, to ensure the children on her caseload are in good hands;

6. An unmarried man in a monastery who has no earthly possessions and no salary to speak of, but finds meaning in communing with his God;

7. A teenager in a foster home who has several close friends and enjoys playing football on his school's team;

8. A man who lives with several pets, enjoys a high salary, and loves his job.

Each of these was pulled from real-world examples of people who are happy. They may not seem like they have it all, but they all have at least one of the ingredients from the list of sources mentioned earlier. We don't need to have everything we want in order to be happy, true happiness can be obtained by finding joy in what we already have, however much or little that may seem.

What are some visions you associate with happiness? Are there any similarities with these dreams?

Importance of Happiness and impact on your life

You might be wondering why happiness is considered such an important aspect of life, as there are many components of a meaningful life.

In some ways, science would agree with you. It appears that life satisfaction, meaning, and well-being can be linked with happiness, but happiness is not necessarily the overarching goal for everyone in life. It is still important because it has some undeniably positive benefits and co-occurring factors.

June Silny at Happify outlines 14 answers to the question, "What's so great about happiness, anyway?"

1. Happy people are more successful in multiple life domains, including marriage, friendship, income, work performance, and health.

2. Happy people get sick less often and experience fewer symptoms when they do get sick.

3. Happy people have more friends and a better support system.

4. Happy people donate more to charity (and giving money to charity makes you happy too).

5. Happy people are more helpful and more likely to volunteer—which also makes you happier!

6. Happy people have an easier time navigating through life since optimism eases pain, sadness, and grief.

7. Happy people have a positive influence on others and encourage them to seek happiness as well, which can act as reinforcement.

8. Happy people engage in deeper and more meaningful conversations.

9. Happy people smile more, which is beneficial to your health.

10. Happy people exercise more often and eat more healthily.

11. Happy people are happy with what they have rather than being jealous of others.

12. Happy people are healthier all around and more likely to be healthy in the future.

13. Happy people live longer than those who are not as happy.

14. Happy people are more productive and more creative, and this effect extends to all those experiencing positive emotions.

How to Train Your Brain for Happiness?

At birth, our genetics provide us with a happiness set point that accounts for about 40% of our happiness. Having enough food, shelter, and safety are 10%.

Then we have 50% that is entirely up to us.

By training our brain through awareness and exercises to think in a happier, more optimistic, and more resilient way, we can effectively train our brains for happiness.

New discoveries in the field of positive psychology show that physical health, psychological well-being, and physiological functioning are all improved by how we learn to "feel good".

THE PATTERNS WE NEED TO "TRAIN OUT" OF OUR BRAINS

1. Perfectionism – Often confused with conscientiousness, which involves appropriate and tangible expectations, perfectionism involves inappropriate levels of expectations and intangible goals. It often produces problems for adults, adolescents, and children.

2. Social comparison – When you compare yourself to others you often find yourself lacking. Healthy social comparison is about finding what you admire in others and learning to strive for those qualities. However, the best comparisons you can make are with yourself. How are you better than you were in the past?

3. Materialism – Attaching your happiness to external things and material wealth is dangerous, as you can lose your happiness if your material circumstances change.

4. Maximizing – Maximizers search for better options even when they are satisfied. This leaves them with little time to be present for the good moments in their lives and with very little gratitude.

Misconceptions about Mind Training

Some of the misconceptions about retraining your brain are simply untrue. Here are a few myths that need debunking:

1. We are products of our genetics so we cannot create change in our brains.

Our minds are malleable. Ten years ago we thought brain pathways were set in early childhood. In fact, we now know that there is huge potential for large changes through to your twenties, and neuroplasticity is still changing throughout one's life.

The myelin sheath that covers your neural pathways gets thicker and stronger the more it is used (think of the plastic protective covering on wires); the more a pathway is used, the stronger the myelin and the faster the neural pathway. Simply put, when you practice feeling grateful, you notice more things to be grateful for.

2. Brain training is brainwashing.

Brainwashing is an involuntary change. If we focus on training our mind to see the glass half full instead of half empty, that is a choice.

3. If we are too happy we run the risk of becoming over optimistic.

There is no such thing as over-optimism, and science shows that brain training for positivity includes practices like mindfulness and gratitude. No one has ever overdosed on these habits.

Living Happily ever after…

If happiness has little to do with having too many resources, then it is an inner state that we have the power to cultivate. The above video even offers specific exercises for you to try. Just by doing them, you are actively rewiring your brain towards calm and happy sensations.

The negativity bias can help us understand how we can activate and "install" positive thinking as part of our core brain chemistry. If you don't have a moment to watch either of these videos now, make time for it later, they are rich with relevant data and tips.

Happiness is the overall subjective experience of our positive emotions. There are many factors which influence our happiness, and ongoing research continues to uncover what makes us the happiest.

Our brain is already designed for happiness. We have caregiving systems in place for eye contact, touch, and vocalizations to let others know we are trustworthy and secure. Our brains also regulate chemicals like oxytocin. People who have more oxytocin trust more readily, have increased tendencies towards monogamy, and exhibit more caregiving behavior. These behaviors reduce stress which lowers production of hormones like cortisol and inhibits the cardiovascular response to stress. This global pursuit of happiness has resulted in measures such as the World Happiness Report, while the World Happiness Database is working to collaborate and consolidate the existing happiness pursuits of different nations.

We are living in a time when the conditions for happiness are known.

"The human brain is wired for happiness and positive connections with others. It is actually possible to experience and learn happiness despite what has been genetically hardwired."

In a world where the focus on happiness is growing and the mirror is turning back towards ourselves, the happiness of the world relies on the happiness within each one of us and how we act, share, and voice the importance of happiness for everyone.

I hope that everything you read until now was informative and that you learned something new about the scientific study of happiness. When it comes to life, it's a fascinating area of research, and new findings are coming out all the time. Make sure you stay up to date on the happiness literature, as the findings can be of great use in helping you to live your life in the best possible way!

Give yourself a pat on the back as we've almost reached our destination! To conclude it all up, we'll be just brushing ourselves with some final thoughts on how to sustain and instill the changes that we discussed over the past few days.

Until then,

Prriya Kaur

"Happiness is not in the mere possession of money; it lies in the joy of achievement, in the thrill of creative effort."

– Franklin D. Roosevelt

Epilogue

Concluding our Journey

Life's a game, Enjoy and Play safe

It is indeed quite a thing to realize how swiftly time passes by. You must be wondering as well, that the journey we started a few days ago is now finally completed. A journey full of interesting conversations and introspections! A handsome amount of time throughout these five days taken out from your busy life - all for yourself. And I believe besides everything else happening around you, life, among all sorts of things, is about giving time to yourself.

When we were embarking upon our journey, I'm sure you must have had a lot of questions meandering all across your head. Perhaps we came across the answers of most of them, leaving no stone unturned, maybe some stones were left. But whatever the case might be, now I'm absolutely confident that you can turn them over as well. The knowledge, the practices, the methodologies that we covered over the span of past few days would remain with you for times to come. And you can implement all the techniques according to the situation or the moment where you'll need them the most.

If we take a look around us and observe what's happening in our lives which are heavily altered by time and space, we'll find out that there's a lot of uncertainty in almost everything. You can only make an effort to shape things according to your way. But hey, don't let this notion of *'whatever's going to happen, would happen'* get in your way of making efforts. Never ever make your approach casual towards anything. Now, that doesn't mean that you need to be serious and grim-faced all the time! Instead, you must perfect the art of striking a balance amongst all sorts of things that interplay to mold your day-to-day life.

We're dwelling in an era where science and technology is thriving at its best. With two of the greatest innovations that've happened in this and the previous century i.e. Social media and the internet respectively can do a whole lot of things that weren't so easy to go for a few decades ago. Now that you know how to make the best out of anything and utilize the resources at your disposal to your advantage, it's about time that you start to live by what you've learnt.

Although, as I mentioned previously, you can shape the course of life to a great extent, the tinge of uncertainty would prevail regardless of anything. What boggles me more than the notion of unpredictability is the limited quantity of time that we've. No, I'm not saying that one should be afraid of the mortal nature of life. Rather we must realize the importance of the precious quantity at our disposal that we often tend to neglect. Thus, it's about *'time'* we start to do those things that we actually wish to do and cherish the experiences that come with it.

Don't wait for the next moment to come – and as one of the popular Shia LaBeouf meme goes *'Just do it!'* Once you get on your desired life track, which I'm sure by now you must have got on or at least have had an idea about. You'll look back only to find out the hurdles that you were thinking would come in your way, were actually the imaginary blockages or obstacles in your mind. And you can always remember this, whenever you want to sign up or go for something new and in case those hindering thoughts are coming back in your mind. In the end it's completely your choice! We're all the masters or prisoners here, of our own design.

With that said, I would like to tell you that you've earned my appreciation for making it all the way until here. I suggest that you keep revisiting the contents in this book so that the crucial mind exercises become a daily part of your life. Mark my words, no one can deter you from your track as long as you understand and have faith in yourself. I hope that this book and my journey instigated a spark within and you're most welcome to adapt anything from my life if you want to.

Through the medium of this book, I tried to propagate a lot of techniques and methodologies that would enable you to channelize your ever withheld power of transitioning from ordinary to extraordinary version of yourself. I want to let you know that I would always be there to help you out, just like I tried to through this book, in and beyond my capacity. And I look forward to hearing from you through email, social media or whatever medium you feel like is best for you, so that I can also amplify the happiness, as you tell me your progress story. May God bless you and I hope that you keep on succeeding ahead in life!

Sending all the positive vibes your way,

May you achieve what you seek for!

And as always - Find yourself, this is the beginning of all wisdom and happiness.

Keep going forth and Good luck, have fun ahead!

- Prriya Kaur

If you would like to get in touch with Prriya Kaur,
visit www.prriya.com

Printed in Great Britain
by Amazon

65025048R00120